THE CARTOON GUIDE
TO PHYSICS

THE
CARTOON
GUIDE TO
PHYSICS

L A R R Y   G O N I C K
AND A R T   H U F F M A N

■ HarperPerennial
A Division of HarperCollinsPublishers

First Harper Perennial edition published 1991.

Illustrations by Lawrence Gonick

Library of Congress Catalog Card Number 90-55499
ISBN 0-06-463618-6

·CONTENTS·

PART ONE: MECHANICS

PART TWO: ELECTRICITY AND MAGNETISM

· PART ONE ·
MECHANICS

CHAPTER ONE
"MOTION"

THE FIRST CONCEPT WE WANT TO UNDERSTAND IS **MOTION**: BIRDS FLYING, PLANETS WHIRLING, TREES FALLING. ALL THE UNIVERSE IS IN MOTION!!

HERE IS A STRAIGHT-LINE COURSE MARKED OFF WITH POSITIVE DISTANCES IN THE FORWARD DIRECTION AND NEGATIVE DISTANCES IN THE REVERSE DIRECTION.

LET'S WATCH MY FELLOW ASTRONAUT **RINGO** AS HE DRIVES A CAR ON THIS COURSE. THE CAR IS MOVING WITH CONSTANT SPEED. THEN IT COVERS THE SAME DISTANCE IN EACH INTERVAL OF TIME, AND WE WRITE:

$$d = v \cdot t$$

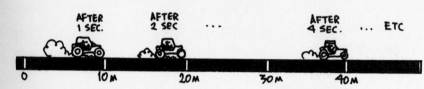

AFTER 1 SEC. AFTER 2 SEC ... AFTER 4 SEC. ... ETC

0   10M   20M   30M   40M

DISTANCE **d** EQUALS SPEED **v** TIMES TIME **t**. IF THE SPEED IS 10 METERS/SEC., THEN IN EACH SECOND RINGO TRAVELS 10 METERS. IN TWO SECONDS HE GOES 20 METERS, IN THREE SECONDS 30 METERS, IN ONE MINUTE 600 METERS
:

AND IN ONE HOUR (3600 S) HE GOES

AND AFTER TWO HOURS, I MAKE A PIT STOP...

3600 S × 10 M/S = 36,000 M =

36 KM.

4

SQUEEEE

IN AN ORDINARY TRIP, YOU ARE ALWAYS SPEEDING UP AND SLOWING DOWN: YOUR SPEED IS NOT CONSTANT. THEN WHAT HAPPENS TO THE EQUATION $d = v \cdot t$? IF v IS CHANGING, WHICH VALUE OF v DO YOU USE?

V CHANGING?

THIS IS TOO CONFUSING.

CHANGE MUST BE AN ILLUSION...

YOU COULD SOLVE THE EQUATION FOR v TO GET
$$v = d/t, \text{ SO}$$

$$v = \frac{\text{INITIAL ODOMETER READING} - \text{FINAL ODOMETER READING}}{\text{ELAPSED TIME}}$$

THIS GIVES THE **AVERAGE** SPEED FOR THE TRIP. IT TOOK THE OLD NATURAL PHILOSOPHERS A LONG TIME TO REALIZE THAT AN OBJECT ALSO HAS AN **INSTANTANEOUS** SPEED, A SPEED AT EACH MOMENT. THAT IS THE NUMBER YOUR SPEEDOMETER MEASURES.

5

PHYSICISTS HAVE FOUND THAT THE DIRECTION OF MOTION IS AS IMPORTANT AS THE SPEED. THEY USE THE WORD

VELOCITY

TO REPRESENT BOTH SPEED AND DIRECTION.

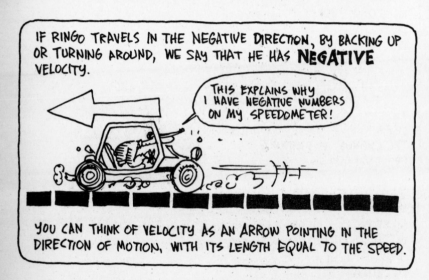

IF RINGO TRAVELS IN THE NEGATIVE DIRECTION, BY BACKING UP OR TURNING AROUND, WE SAY THAT HE HAS **NEGATIVE** VELOCITY.

THIS EXPLAINS WHY I HAVE NEGATIVE NUMBERS ON MY SPEEDOMETER!

YOU CAN THINK OF VELOCITY AS AN ARROW POINTING IN THE DIRECTION OF MOTION, WITH ITS LENGTH EQUAL TO THE SPEED.

MORE GENERALLY, IF RINGO DRIVES IN ANY DIRECTION, WE REPRESENT HIS VELOCITY BY AN ARROW — FOR EXAMPLE, $V = 32$ m/sec AT 28° EAST OF NORTH.

WHEN AN OBJECT'S VELOCITY
CHANGES, WE SAY THAT IT

ACCELERATES

WE DEFINE ACCELERATION AS
THE CHANGE IN VELOCITY
PER UNIT TIME:

$$a = \frac{v}{t}$$

THIS IS SIMILAR TO THE
DEFINITION OF SPEED, AS
THE CHANGE IN DISTANCE
PER UNIT TIME.

LET'S RIDE WITH RINGO AGAIN. HIS CAR HAS A LINEAR
SPEEDOMETER, WITH NEGATIVE READINGS FOR BACKING UP—
A "VELOCITOMETER."
THEN ACCELERATION
IS NOTHING BUT
THE VELOCITY OF
THE INDICATOR
NEEDLE!!

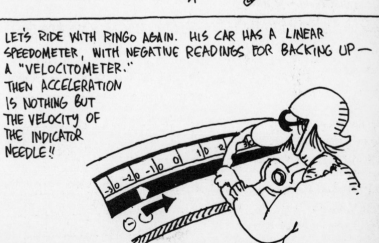

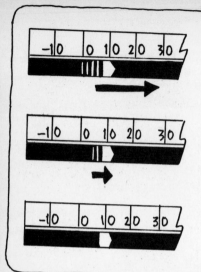

IF THE VELOCITY IS CHANGING RAPIDLY, WE HAVE A BIG ACCELERATION.

IF THE VELOCITY CHANGES SLOWLY, ACCELERATION IS SMALL.

AND IF RINGO MAINTAINS A STEADY SPEED, HIS ACCELERATION IS ZERO.

NOW WATCH AS RINGO ACCELERATES SMOOTHLY FROM 0 TO 50 km/hr. IN 5 SEC. THE SPEEDOMETER INDICATOR MOVES WITH **CONSTANT SPEED**, SO HERE **ACCELERATION IS A CONSTANT,** AND WE CALCULATE:

$$a = \frac{\text{FINAL SPEED} - \text{INITIAL SPEED}}{\text{ELAPSED TIME}} = \frac{50 \text{ KM/H}}{5 \text{ S}}$$

$$= \frac{50 \text{ KM/H}}{5 \text{ S}} \times \left(\frac{1 \text{ H}}{3600 \text{ S}}\right)\left(\frac{1000 \text{ M}}{1 \text{ KM}}\right) = 13.89 \text{ M/S}^2$$

THESE TWO FACTORS ARE BOTH EQUAL TO 1 — WE INTRODUCE THEM TO CONVERT HOURS TO SECONDS AND METERS TO KILOMETERS.

NOTE THAT THE UNITS OF ACCELERATION ARE M/S² — METERS PER SECOND PER SECOND!

8

DID YOU NOTICE ANOTHER EFFECT WHEN RINGO WAS ACCELERATING? WHENEVER THE CAR ACCELERATED FORWARD, RINGO WAS PUSHED BACK INTO HIS SEAT.

IN GENERAL,

FORCES ARE ASSOCIATED WITH ACCELERATION

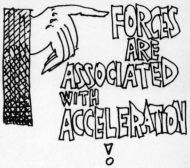

NOW RINGO APPLIES THE BRAKES.

MUST BE DOWN HERE SOMEWHERE...

THE CAR SLOWS DOWN, AND RINGO FEELS A FORCE PUSHING HIM FORWARD.

IN THIS BRAKING, OR **DECELERATION** SITUATION, THE SPEEDOMETER INDICATOR MOVES TO THE LEFT— I.E., ITS VELOCITY IS NEGATIVE.

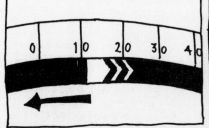

0   10   20   30   40

SO THE CAR HAS NEGATIVE ACCELERATION WHEN IT SLOWS DOWN.

RUMBLE RUMBLE RUMBLE

DID YOU NOTICE THAT THE ACCELERATION IS OPPOSITE TO THE DIRECTION OF THE FORCE YOU FEEL?

I FEEL SO MUCH...

THE CAR HAS NEGATIVE ACCELERATION IF IT IS SLOWING DOWN FROM A POSITIVE VELOCITY, OR IF IT'S SPEEDING UP IN THE NEGATIVE DIRECTION.

EITHER WAY, THE SPEEDOMETER IS MOVING TO THE LEFT!

WE CAN USE THE ACCELERATION FORCES TO MAKE AN INDICATOR OF ACCELERATION — AN **ACCELEROMETER.** WE SIMPLY SUSPEND A MASS BY A STRING FROM RINGO'S ROLL BAR.

WHEN HE ACCELERATES FORWARD, THE MASS SWINGS BACK TO AN ANGLE FROM THE VERTICAL.

WITH NEGATIVE ACCELERATION, THE MASS MOVES TO A FORWARD ANGLE.

THE MASS MOVES IN A DIRECTION OPPOSITE TO THE ACCELERATION, AND THE ANGLE EVEN GIVES A MEASURE OF THE ACCELERATION.

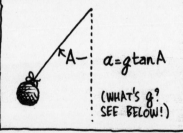

$a = g \tan A$

(WHAT'S g? SEE BELOW!)

HERE IS ANOTHER ACCELERATION SITUATION: RINGO DRIVES AT A CONSTANT SPEED OF 20 KM/HR AROUND A CIRCULAR TRACK.

ALTHOUGH THE SPEEDOMETER ISN'T CHANGING, RINGO FEELS A FORCE PUSHING HIM TO THE OUTSIDE OF THE CURVE, AND THE ACCELEROMETER HANGS TO THE OUTSIDE OF THE CURVE.

HERE THE "SPEED OF THE SPEEDOMETER" TEST FAILS. EVEN THOUGH RINGO'S SPEED ISN'T CHANGING, HIS **VELOCITY** IS — BECAUSE ITS DIRECTION IS CHANGING AS HE TRAVELS AROUND...

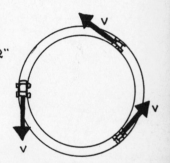

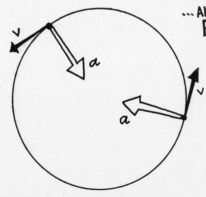

...AND WE HAVE AN ACCELERATION **PERPENDICULAR** TO THE MOTION, OPPOSITE TO THE FORCES HE FEELS. THE ACCELEROMETER MEASURES THE ACCELERATION CORRECTLY. SO: WHEN AN OBJECT MOVES IN A CIRCLE, WITH CONSTANT SPEED, ITS ACCELERATION IS TOWARD THE **CENTER OF THE CIRCLE.**

ACCELERATION IS NOT AN EASY CONCEPT,
BUT IT IS A BASIC ONE IN PHYSICS.
MOST MOTIONS IN THE WORLD
ARE NOT SIMPLE: THE SPEED
AND DIRECTION ARE ALWAYS
CHANGING. IN OTHER WORDS,
THEY ARE ACCELERATING!!

DIRECTION CONSTANT,
SPEED CHANGING

SPEED CONSTANT,
DIRECTION CHANGING

SPEED
AND
DIRECTION
CHANGING

VELOCITY IS GIVEN BY THE BASIC
EQUATION

$$v = d/t$$

VELOCITY IS THE RATE OF CHANGE
OF DISTANCE. ACCELERATION IS
THE RATE OF CHANGE OF VELOCITY.
EVEN ACCELERATION CAN BE
CHANGING!

MINE IS
ABOUT TO
CHANGE
ABRUPTLY!

12

BUT IN BEGINNING PHYSICS, WE USUALLY STICK TO **CONSTANT ACCELERATION** SITUATIONS.

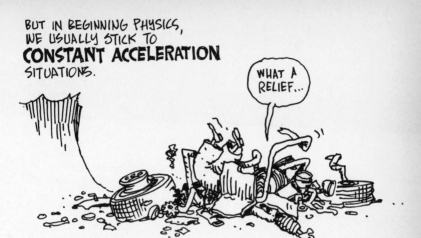

WHAT A RELIEF...

SUPPOSE YOU START FROM REST AND UNDERGO CONSTANT ACCELERATION a FOR A PERIOD OF TIME t. HOW FAR DO YOU GO IN THIS TIME?

t=0
v=0

v=at

WELL, YOUR INITIAL SPEED IS ZERO, AND IT INCREASED UNIFORMLY. TO $v = at$ IN TIME t. SO YOUR **AVERAGE** SPEED DURING THIS INTERVAL WAS:

$$v_{AVERAGE} = \frac{0 + at}{2} = \frac{1}{2}at$$

THEN THE DISTANCE TRAVELED d IS THE AVERAGE SPEED TIMES TIME t, OR

$$d = \frac{1}{2}at \cdot t$$

$$d = \frac{1}{2}at^2$$

FOR EXAMPLE, SUPPOSE RINGO ACCELERATES FROM 0 TO 50 $\frac{KM}{HR}$ IN 5 SEC. LET'S SEE HOW FAR HE GOES. THIS PROBLEM HAS TWO STEPS. FIRST, WE MUST FIND THE ACCELERATION. THIS WE ALREADY DID ABOVE, FINDING $a = 13.89$ m/sec², SO

$$d = \frac{1}{2}at^2$$

$$= \frac{1}{2}(13.89 \text{ m/s}^2) \cdot (5_s)$$

$$= 173.6 \text{ METERS}$$

13

FALLING

IS ANOTHER COMMON KIND OF MOTION.

OH, NO! NOT AGAIN!

TRY DROPPING SOMETHING, THIS BOOK, FOR EXAMPLE! DID IT MOVE AT CONSTANT SPEED? IT PROBABLY HAPPENED SO FAST, YOU COULDN'T TELL.

GALILEO

(1564-1642) ALSO WONDERED ABOUT THIS PROBLEM.

GALILEO FIGURED OUT A WAY TO SLOW DOWN THE FALLING MOTION, SO IT COULD BE STUDIED AT LEISURE. HIS APPARATUS? AN **INCLINED PLANE.**

GALILEO ROLLED MANY OBJECTS DOWN INCLINED PLANES, USING HIS OWN PULSE AS A CLOCK.

"SUPER SLO-MO!"

HOW DO WE KNOW THAT ROLLING DOWN A SLOPE IS LIKE FALLING, ONLY SLOWER? AH, THERE IS GALILEO'S GENIUS!! AS HE TILTS THE PLANE STEEPER AND STEEPER, THE MOTION BECOMES FREE FALL!

GALILEO FOUND THAT THE DISTANCE A BALL ROLLS INCREASES WITH THE SQUARE OF THE ELAPSED TIME — FITTING THE FORMULA

$$d = \frac{1}{2}at^2.$$

SO: **OBJECTS FALL WITH CONSTANT ACCELERATION.**

GALILEO ALSO WONDERED HOW AN OBJECT'S RATE OF FALLING IS AFFECTED BY ITS **MASS.** "EVERYONE KNOWS" THAT A BRICK FALLS FASTER THAN A FEATHER.

SO THIS FEATHER SHOULD SLOW MY FALL?

BUT GALILEO'S EXPERIMENTS PRODUCED A SURPRISE: NEGLECTING AIR RESISTANCE,

ALL OBJECTS FALL WITH THE SAME ACCELERATION, REGARDLESS OF MASS.

A FEATHER HAS A LOT OF AIR RESISTANCE, AND NORMALLY FLUTTERS SLOWLY, BUT IN A VACUUM, AS ON THE MOON, IT DROPS LIKE A BRICK.

WE CAN DUPLICATE THE EXPERIMENT HERE ON EARTH, INSIDE A CONTAINER WITH THE AIR PUMPED OUT.

FROM CAREFUL MEASUREMENT, WE HAVE DETERMINED THIS RATE OF ACCELERATION: NEAR THE SURFACE OF THE EARTH, ALL OBJECTS FALL WITH A CONSTANT ACCELERATION g EQUAL TO

$$32 \text{ ft/sec}^2$$
$$= 9.8 \text{ m/sec}^2$$

(NEGLECTING AIR RESISTANCE).

(INCIDENTALLY, **EINSTEIN** [1879-1955] REASONED THAT BECAUSE ALL OBJECTS MOVE THE SAME IN A GRAVITATIONAL FIELD, GRAVITY MUST BE A PROPERTY OF **SPACE** AND **TIME** RATHER THAN OF THE OBJECTS THEMSELVES.

TO MAKE THIS MORE CONCRETE, LET'S DROP A BLOCK OF IT (CONCRETE, THAT IS) FROM THIS ROOFTOP.

THIS IS MOTION WITH CONSTANT ACCELERATION g. SO VELOCITY INCREASES PROPORTIONALLY TO TIME:

$$v = g \cdot t$$

AFTER ONE SECOND OF FALLING, IT IS GOING

$$(9.8 \text{ m/s}^2) \cdot (1 \text{ s}) = 9.8 \text{ m/s}$$

AFTER 2 SECONDS, ITS SPEED IS

$$(9.8 \text{ m/s}^2)(2 \text{ s}) = 19.6 \text{ m/s}$$

ETC.—

HOW FAR DOES IT FALL IN TIME t? APPLY OUR FORMULA

$$d = \frac{1}{2}g \cdot t^2$$

AFTER ONE SECOND, IT HAS FALLEN

$$\frac{1}{2}(9.8 \text{ m/s}^2) \cdot (1 \text{ s})$$

$$= 4.9 \text{ meters}$$

AFTER 2 SECONDS, THE DISTANCE IS

$$\frac{1}{2}(9.8 \text{ m/s}^2)(2 \text{ s})$$

$$= 19.6 \text{ meters}.$$

t	v	d
0	0	0
0.5	4.9 m/s	1.3 m
1	9.8 m/s	4.9 m
2	19.6 m/s	19.6 m
3	29.4 m/s	44.1 m
4	39.2 m/s	78.4 m

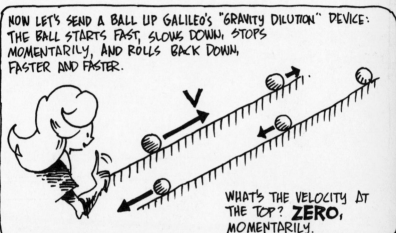

NOW LET'S SEND A BALL UP GALILEO'S "GRAVITY DILUTION" DEVICE: THE BALL STARTS FAST, SLOWS DOWN, STOPS MOMENTARILY, AND ROLLS BACK DOWN, FASTER AND FASTER.

WHAT'S THE VELOCITY AT THE TOP? **ZERO,** MOMENTARILY.

BUT WHAT'S THE **ACCELERATION** AT THE TOP? NOT ZERO! THE ACCELERATION IS CONSTANT THROUGHOUT THE WHOLE MOTION. THE ACCELERATION SLOWS THE BALL DOWN AS IT ROLLS UP AND SPEEDS IT UP AS IT ROLLS DOWN. SIMILARLY, THE ROCK THROWN INTO THE AIR ALWAYS HAS ACCELERATION **g DOWNWARD.**

17

· CHAPTER 2 ·
THE APPLE AND THE MOON

ON ORDER TO UNDERSTAND THE MOON'S MOTION, AND ALL THE OTHER MOTION AROUND US, WE FIRST ASK THE QUESTION: WHAT DO OBJECTS DO WHEN **NO** FORCE IS ACTING?

FOR CENTURIES, PHYSICS SLEPT IN THE SHADOW OF

ARISTOTLE

(384-322 B.C.). ARISTOTLE BELIEVED THAT THE "NATURAL" MOTION OF **CELESTIAL** OBJECTS (MOON, STARS) WAS **CIRCULAR**, WHILE **TERRESTRIAL** OBJECTS (APPLES, ROCKS, YOU) TEND "NATURALLY" TO **FALL**.

NOTICE THAT IF THE MOON NATURALLY MOVES IN A CIRCLE, WE DON'T NEED ANY GRAVITY TO EXPLAIN ITS MOTION.

IT'S JUST "NATURAL".

AS FOR EARTHLY OBJECTS, ARISTOTLE THOUGHT THAT AFTER FALLING, THEY COME TO REST, UNLESS SOME FORCE PUSHES THEM SIDEWAYS.

HASN'T MOVED YET!

AND WE INSTINCTIVELY AGREE WITH HIM! IT DOES SEEM THAT A FORCE IS NEEDED TO MAINTAIN MOTION, LIKE A MOTOR PROPELLING A CAR.

ROAR

WHEN THE ENGINE IS CUT OFF, THE CAR GRADUALLY... ROLLS... TO... A .... HALT....

CHUFF

CLANK PWEET

TINK SHUDDER

IT TOOK THE GENIUS OF GALILEO TO CLAIM THAT

NO FORCE

IS NEEDED TO KEEP AN OBJECT IN

UNIFORM, STRAIGHT-LINE MOTION.

SO BUZZ OFF!

19

GALILEO'S BRAINSTORM
WAS TO SEE THAT FORCES
CHANGE THE MOTION
OF OBJECTS. LEFT
ALONE, THINGS WOULD
TRAVEL IN A STRAIGHT
LINE FOREVER. IT IS
THE FORCE OF **FRICTION**
THAT SLOWS THEM DOWN.

WE CAN CONVINCE OURSELVES OF THIS IDEA WITH A SIMPLE
APPARATUS CONSISTING OF A FLEXIBLE RUBBER MAT:

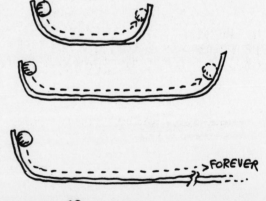

A ROLLING BALL
TENDS TO REACH
THE SAME
HEIGHT ON THE
OTHER SIDE...
AND IF THERE
WERE NO OTHER
SIDE, IT WOULD
ROLL ON FOREVER,
IF NOT FOR
FRICTION.

ISAAC **NEWTON** (1642-1727) SUMMARIZED GALILEO'S
IDEA AS **NEWTON'S FIRST LAW:**

HEAR YE! HEAR YE!

AN OBJECT AT REST
TENDS TO STAY AT
REST. AN OBJECT
IN MOTION TENDS
TO CONTINUE IN
MOTION AT
CONSTANT SPEED
IN A STRAIGHT
LINE.

(HE ALSO SAID: "IF I
HAVE SEEN FAR, IT IS
BECAUSE I HAVE
STOOD ON THE SHOULDERS
OF GIANTS," MEANING
GALILEO OF COURSE...)

IN THE TERMINOLOGY WE DEVELOPED IN CHAPTER ONE,
WE WOULD SAY THAT WHEN THERE ARE NO FORCES,
OBJECTS MOVE WITH **CONSTANT VELOCITY.**

ZIP

THE PROPERTY OF OBJECTS THAT MAKES THEM "TEND" TO OBEY NEWTON'S FIRST LAW, WE CALL **INERTIA.** INERTIA IS RESISTANCE TO CHANGES IN MOTION.

WHATEVER "ERT" IS, I'M IN IT!

THE AMOUNT OF INERTIA A BODY HAS IS MEASURED BY ITS **MASS.** MASSIVE THINGS HAVE LOTS OF INERTIA, MEANING THAT A LARGE FORCE IS REQUIRED TO CHANGE THEIR MOTION.

SMALL INERTIA

BIG INERTIA

WE SAID PREVIOUSLY THAT WHEN RINGO RIDES IN A CAR THAT ACCELERATES, HE FEELS FORCES.

THESE ARE THE FORCES THE CAR HAS TO EXERT ON RINGO TO OVERCOME HIS INERTIA AND ACCELERATE HIM.

MR. NEWTON WILL SUMMARIZE:

BREAKER ONE.NINE: FORCE OVERCOMES INERTIA AND PRODUCES ACCELERATION. DO YOU READ?

22

NEWTON PUT THIS RELATIONSHIP AMONG FORCE, MASS, AND ACCELERATION INTO MATHEMATICAL FORM WITH NEWTON'S

SECOND LAW:

$$F = m \cdot a$$

OR $a = F/m$

OR, THEN AGAIN, $m = F/a$

THE MORE FORCE ON AN OBJECT, THE MORE IT ACCELERATES. BUT THE MORE MASSIVE IT IS, THE MORE IT RESISTS ACCELERATION.

UNH!

NOW LET'S LOOK AT THE MOON AGAIN. IT GOES IN A CIRCLE AROUND THE EARTH, OR NEARLY SO. AS WE HAVE SEEN, THINGS THAT MOVE IN A CIRCLE ARE ACCELERATING. THEREFORE, IT HAS A FORCE ACTING ON IT. IT MUST BE THAT **THE EARTH IS PULLING ON THE MOON.**

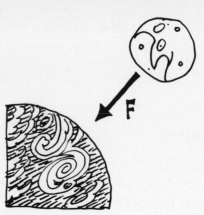

WE KNOW THAT THE EARTH PULLS ON OBJECTS NEAR ITS SURFACE, CAUSING THEM TO ACCELERATE DOWNWARD.

THE SAME FORCE, **GRAVITY,** ACTS ON THE MOON, PULLING IT AWAY FROM THE STRAIGHT LINE IT WOULD HAVE TAKEN IN THE ABSENCE OF GRAVITY.

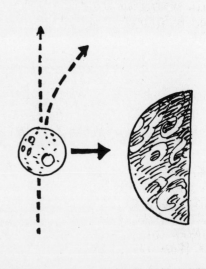

WHEN RELEASED IN MID-AIR, AN APPLE WOULD HAVE REMAINED AT REST (ITS "NATURAL" MOTION), IF NOT FOR THE EFFECT OF GRAVITY MAKING IT FALL.

NOT TO MENTION MY HAIR!

SIMILARLY, IN THE ABSENCE OF GRAVITY (OR OTHER FORCES), THE MOON WOULD CONTINUE ALONG A STRAIGHT LINE AT UNIFORM SPEED. BUT GRAVITY DOES PULL IT, ACCELERATING THE MOON TOWARD THE EARTH. **THE MOON IS FALLING —** FALLING AWAY FROM ITS NATURAL "FIRST LAW" STRAIGHT-LINE MOTION.

IN ONE SEC., THE MOON FALLS ABOUT 1 mm AWAY FROM A STRAIGHT-LINE PATH

IN ONE SEC., AN APPLE FALLS 4.9 m NEAR THE EARTH'S SURFACE.

THE MOON DOESN'T FALL AS MUCH AS THE APPLE, BECAUSE THE EARTH'S GRAVITY IS WEAKER OUT THERE, FAR FROM THE EARTH.

STOP FOR A MOMENT AND CONSIDER WHAT NEWTON ACCOMPLISHED. THE MOTION OF THE APPLE AND THE MOON OBEY THE SAME LAWS. HEAVENLY BODIES BEHAVE NO DIFFERENTLY FROM EARTHLY ONES. NEWTON'S LAWS ARE—

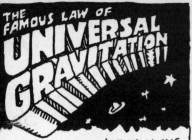

THE FAMOUS LAW OF **UNIVERSAL GRAVITATION**

FOR GRAVITY NEWTON'S FORMULA WAS:

$$F = G \cdot \frac{M \cdot m}{r^2}$$

THE GRAVITATIONAL FORCE BETWEEN TWO MASSES M AND m IS PROPORTIONAL TO THE PRODUCT OF THE MASSES AND INVERSELY PROPORTIONAL TO THE SQUARE OF THE DISTANCE r BETWEEN THEM.

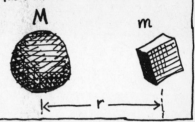

EVERYTHING IN THE UNIVERSE ATTRACTS EVERYTHING ELSE!! THE EARTH ATTRACTS THE MOON, THE MOON ATTRACTS THE EARTH, YOU ATTRACT ME...

OH?

OF COURSE, IF THE MASSES ARE AS SMALL AS YOURS AND MINE, THE FORCE IS SMALL.

VERY.

CHOFF EAT SWALP

BBQ RIBS

ANY STRONGER NOW?

NOT MEASURABLY...

THAT NUMBER G IN THE FORMULA IS A CONSTANT OF NATURE THAT INDICATES HOW STRONG THE GRAVITATIONAL FORCE IS. TO MEASURE G, YOU WOULD HAVE TO PERFORM AN EXPERIMENT TO MEASURE THE ATTRACTION BETWEEN TWO KNOWN MASSES.

27

GRAVITY GETS WEAKER WITH DISTANCE. WE SAW THAT THE DISTANT MOON FALLS SLOWER THAN AN EARTHBOUND APPLE. ANOTHER EFFECT OF THIS **INVERSE·SQUARE LAW** IS THE **TIDE**, THE TWICE·DAILY RISE AND FALL OF OCEAN WATER.

THE WATER DIRECTLY UNDER THE MOON IS CLOSER TO THE MOON THAN THE CENTER OF THE EARTH IS... SO THE MOON'S GRAVITY PULLS HARDER ON THE WATER, AND THE WATER "HEAPS UP" UNDER THE MOON. AND SINCE THE CENTER OF THE EARTH IS CLOSER TO THE MOON THAN THE WATER ON THE **OPPOSITE** SIDE OF THE EARTH, THE MOON PULLS THE EARTH AWAY FROM THAT WATER, SO IT HEAPS UP TOO!

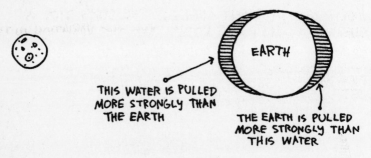

THIS WATER IS PULLED MORE STRONGLY THAN THE EARTH

EARTH

THE EARTH IS PULLED MORE STRONGLY THAN THIS WATER

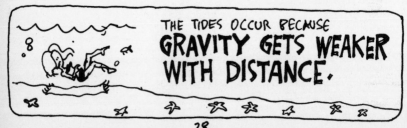

THE TIDES OCCUR BECAUSE **GRAVITY GETS WEAKER WITH DISTANCE.**

THE SUN ALSO CAUSES TIDES IN THE SAME WAY, BUT LESS SO, BECAUSE OF THE SUN'S GREATER DISTANCE. AT FULL MOON AND NEW MOON EACH MONTH, THE SUN IS IN LINE WITH THE MOON AND THE EARTH. THEN THE SUN AND MOON TOGETHER PRODUCE EXTRA-HIGH AND EXTRA-LOW TIDES. THESE ARE THE TWICE-MONTHLY **SPRING TIDES.** *

FULL MOON:

MOON   WATER

EARTH

NEW MOON

AT FIRST QUARTER AND LAST QUARTER, THE SUN AND MOON ARE AT RIGHT ANGLES. THE SUN'S TIDE IS SUBTRACTED FROM THE MOON'S, AND THE VARIATION IN TIDES IS LESS. THESE ARE THE **NEAP TIDES.**

FIRST QUARTER

LAST QUARTER

(NOT TO SCALE!!)

* THESE HAVE NOTHING TO DO WITH THE SPRING SEASON.

NOW LET'S THINK ABOUT GRAVITY'S EFFECTS ON THINGS NEAR THE EARTH, YOU, FOR EXAMPLE. THE GRAVITATIONAL FORCE ON YOU IS YOUR **WEIGHT**.

BOO!

W

YOU WOULD WEIGH LESS IF:

YOU WENT ON A DIET AND LOST MASS.

THE EARTH HAD LESS MASS (OR YOU WERE ON THE MOON).

YOU WERE FARTHER FROM THE EARTH; UP ON THE ROOF, YOU ACTUALLY WEIGH SLIGHTLY LESS.

NOW YOU JUMP OFF THE ROOF — WHAT IS YOUR ACCELERATION? NOTE THAT WE NOW HAVE TWO WAYS TO EXPRESS THE GRAVITATIONAL FORCE ON YOU:

FROM NEWTON'S SECOND LAW:	FROM UNIVERSAL GRAVITATION:
$F = mg$	$F = G\dfrac{Mm}{r^2}$

SETTING THESE EQUAL, WE FIND:

$$mg = G\frac{Mm}{r^2}, \text{ SO } g = G\frac{M}{r^2}$$

THIS LAST FORMULA SHOWS HOW g IS RELATED TO THE FUNDAMENTAL CONSTANT G AND THE EARTH'S MASS AND RADIUS. NOTE THAT m, YOUR MASS, CANCELS OUT. g DOESN'T DEPEND ON YOUR MASS!

30

THE FORCE THE EARTH EXERTS ON YOU $W = mg$ SHOWS THE DISTINCTION BETWEEN **WEIGHT** AND **MASS.**

MASS, **m**, IS THE QUANTITY OF MATTER IN AN OBJECT. MASS MEASURES (1) HOW MUCH GRAVITY IT EXERTS ON OTHER OBJECTS AND (2) HOW MUCH IT RESISTS ACCELERATION, HOW MUCH INERTIA IT HAS.

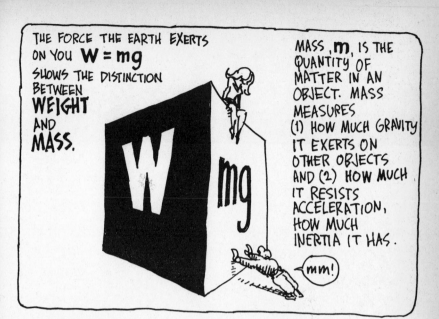

mm!

WEIGHT, **W**, IS THE AMOUNT OF GRAVITATIONAL PULL ON THE OBJECT. WEIGHT VARIES ACCORDING TO WHERE YOU ARE: IN DEEP SPACE, YOUR WEIGHT MIGHT BE ZERO, BUT YOUR MASS IS THE SAME WHEREVER YOU GO!

INTERPLANETARY WEIGHT LOSS CENTER "WE REMIND YOU OF A DONUT."

COULD WORK!

WE EVEN MEASURE WEIGHT AND MASS IN DIFFERENT UNITS. IN THE METRIC SYSTEM, THE **GRAM** IS THE UNIT OF MASS, WHILE THE **NEWTON** IS THE UNIT OF WEIGHT. A PERSON "MASSING" 50 kg (1 kg = 1000 grams) HAS A WEIGHT

$$W = mg$$
$$= (50 \text{ kg}) \cdot (9.8 \text{ m/sec}^2)$$
$$= 490 \text{ NEWTONS.}$$

IT IS TECHNICALLY INCORRECT TO SAY THAT SOMETHING "WEIGHS" 50 kg. WEIGHT IS STATED IN UNITS OF FORCE, NEWTONS.

CONFUSING? LISTEN TO THIS: IN THE ENGLISH SYSTEM, THE UNIT OF FORCE IS THE **POUND**, WHILE THE UNIT OF MASS IS THE **SLUG**.

A PERSON WEIGHING 160 POUNDS HAS A MASS

$$m = \frac{W}{g} = \frac{160 \text{ POUNDS}}{32 \text{ ft/sec}^2}$$

$$= 5 \text{ SLUGS.}$$

AT LAST, A UNIT WITH A BEAUTIFUL NAME!

✢ CHAPTER 3 ✢
PROJECTILES

SO FAR, WE HAVE
BEEN WEIGHING
AND DROPPING
THINGS.

NOW LET'S SHOOT SOME!

IN ORDER TO UNTANGLE HORIZONTAL AND VERTICAL MOTIONS?

THE SIMPLEST PROJECTILE MOTION IS TO PROJECT SOMETHING
SIDEWAYS: DRIVING A CAR OFF A CLIFF OR SHOOTING A
BULLET HORIZONTALLY. THE KEY TO UNDERSTANDING
THIS MOTION IS TO REALIZE THAT GRAVITY ACTS ONLY
VERTICALLY. IT AFFECTS ONLY THE **DOWNWARD**
PART OF THE MOTION.

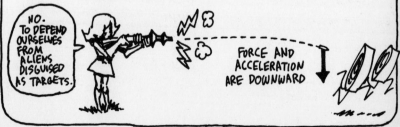

NO. TO DEPEND OURSELVES FROM ALIENS DISGUISED AS TARGETS.

FORCE AND ACCELERATION ARE DOWNWARD

THIS FACT IMMEDIATELY ANSWERS A FAMOUS QUESTION: IF RINGO DROPS A BULLET AT THE SAME MOMENT AS I SHOOT A BULLET HORIZONTALLY, WHICH BULLET HITS THE GROUND FIRST? (WE START AT THE SAME HEIGHT.)

1...2...3...

THEY REACH THE GROUND AT THE SAME TIME, BECAUSE THEY **FALL AT THE SAME RATE.** THE HORIZONTAL MOTION HAS NO EFFECT ON THE VERTICAL MOTION!

EXAMPLE: SUPPOSE I FIRE THE BULLET FROM A SHOULDER HEIGHT OF 4 FT. THEN THE DISTANCE FALLEN IS

$$d = \tfrac{1}{2}gt^2, \quad \text{SO}$$
$$4\,\text{ft} = \tfrac{1}{2}(32\,\text{ft/sec}^2)\cdot t^2$$
$$\text{SO} \quad t = \sqrt{1\,\text{sec}^2/4} = \tfrac{1}{2}\,\text{sec}.$$

BIP

SAME DOWNWARD ACCELERATION AND VELOCITY.

IF THE BULLET'S HORIZONTAL SPEED IS 1000 ft/sec, THEN IT GOES 500 FEET IN $\tfrac{1}{2}$ sec

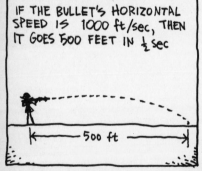

500 ft

NOW HERE'S ANOTHER QUESTION: WHAT HAPPENS IF THE GUN IS FIRED UPWARD AT AN ANGLE?

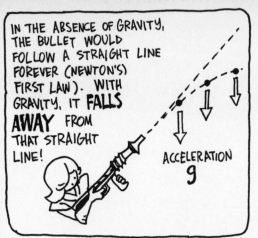

IN THE ABSENCE OF GRAVITY, THE BULLET WOULD FOLLOW A STRAIGHT LINE FOREVER (NEWTON'S FIRST LAW). WITH GRAVITY, IT **FALLS AWAY** FROM THAT STRAIGHT LINE!

ACCELERATION **g**

...WHICH BRINGS US TO A THOUGHT-EXPERIMENT: CALLED

"MONKEY AND HUNTER."

DOWN WITH ANIMAL EXPERIMENTS!

A HUNTER AIMS HIS GUN DIRECTLY AT A MONKEY HANGING FROM A TREE.

THE MONKEY CLEVERLY RELEASES HIS GRIP AT THE EXACT MOMENT THE HUNTER FIRES THE GUN. WHAT HAPPENS?

BWOM

POOR MONKEY!! IT DOESN'T UNDERSTAND THE INDEPENDENCE OF FALLING AND FORWARD MOTION! BUT YOU DO — SO YOU CAN SEE THAT THE BULLET WILL ALWAYS HIT THE MONKEY!

IN CASE THE BULLET GOES FAST, THE BULLET AND MONKEY FALL ONLY A LITTLE WAY.

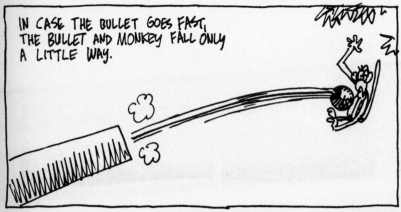

IF THE BULLET IS SLOW, THEY FALL FARTHER, **BUT** THEY FALL THE SAME DISTANCE FROM THE SAME STRAIGHT LINE!!

36

CHAPTER 4
SATELLITE MOTION AND WEIGHTLESSNESS

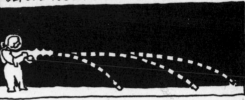

NOW WE'RE ON THE MOON, WHERE THERE'S NO AIR RESISTANCE. WATCH AS I FIRE BULLETS HORIZONTALLY WITH GREATER AND GREATER SPEED. EACH BULLET FALLS TO THE GROUND IN THE SAME TIME — THE HORIZONTAL MOTION DOESN'T AFFECT THE FALLING RATE — BUT THE FASTER BULLETS GO FARTHER BEFORE PLOWING INTO THE MOON.

THE GUN IS 4 FEET OFF THE GROUND. ON EARTH, THE BULLET FALLS IN $\frac{1}{2}$ SEC., BUT HERE, WHERE GRAVITY IS WEAKER, IT TAKES 1.2 SEC. (AS LONG AS THE GROUND IS LEVEL).

BUT AS THE BULLETS GO FARTHER, SOMETHING NEW HAPPENS: THE MOON ISN'T FLAT, IT'S ROUND!! THE GROUND STARTS CURVING DOWN UNDER THE BULLET AND AWAY FROM IT.

EVENTUALLY, AS I FIRE FASTER AND FASTER, BY THE TIME THE BULLET HAS FALLEN 4 FT., THE GROUND HAS CURVED 4 FT. DOWN AND THE BULLET IS **STILL** 4 FT. HIGH! BY THE TIME IT FALLS ANOTHER 4 FT., SO HAS THE GROUND!

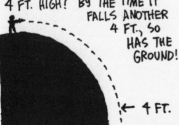

← 4 FT.

THE BULLET IS NOW IN A 4-FOOT-HIGH **ORBIT** AROUND THE MOON. IT IS FALLING CONTINUALLY, BUT THE GROUND IS STEADILY CURVING AWAY BENEATH IT.

OF COURSE, THIS WORKS ONLY WHEN THERE IS NO AIR RESISTANCE (AND NO 4·FT·HIGH OBSTACLES!) TO SLOW THE BULLET, BUT THE EXPERIMENT ILLUSTRATES THE PRINCIPLE OF SATELLITE MOTION. FROM EARTH WE LAUNCH SATELLITES ABOVE THE ATMOSPHERE WITH ROCKETS, THEN TILT THEM OVER AND GIVE THEM ENOUGH **HORIZONTAL** SPEED SO THAT THE EARTH CURVES AWAY FROM THEM AS THEY FALL.

SIMILARLY, OUR NATURAL SATELLITE, THE MOON, FALLS CONTINUALLY, BUT ITS FORWARD MOTION CARRIES IT ALONG SO IT REMAINS THE SAME HEIGHT ABOVE EARTH. (THE MOON'S ORBIT IS CIRCULAR, OR NEARLY SO.)

NOW LET'S GO UP IN THE SPACE SHUTTLE. AS WE REACH ORBITAL SPEED AND I CUT OFF THE ENGINES, THE ONLY FORCE ON US IS **GRAVITY,** AND WE FALL TOWARD EARTH.

WOOAH!

BUT THE SAME IS TRUE OF THE SHUTTLE ITSELF. IT'S ALSO FALLING, AND WITH THE SAME ACCELERATION

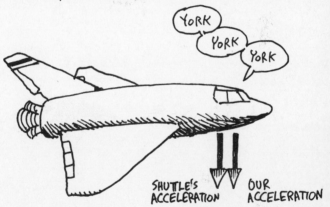

YORK
YORK
YORK

SHUTTLE'S ACCELERATION   OUR ACCELERATION

SO THERE IS NO NO RELATIVE MOTION BETWEEN US AND THE SHIP, AND WE FLOAT FREELY INSIDE, WEIGHTLESS !!

STAY IN THE BAG!

IF YOU RELEASE AN APPLE IN THE FALLING SHUTTLE, IT HANGS IN MID-AIR. GIVE IT A NUDGE AND IT TRAVELS IN A STRAIGHT LINE. IT OBEYS NEWTON'S FIRST LAW!

WHENEVER THE ONLY FORCE ON THE CRAFT IS GRAVITY, WHETHER IT'S COASTING UP, FALLING DOWN, OR IN ORBIT, OBJECTS INSIDE ARE **WEIGHTLESS.**

THE SCALE KEEPS FLOATING AWAY...

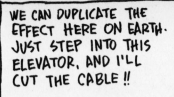

WE CAN DUPLICATE THE EFFECT HERE ON EARTH. JUST STEP INTO THIS ELEVATOR, AND I'LL CUT THE CABLE!!

YOU'LL ONLY BE WEIGHTLESS A LITTLE WHILE!

OH, GOOD.

THUS, ALTHOUGH GRAVITY PRODUCES ACCELERATION, NO **ACCELERATION FORCES** ARE FELT WITHIN THE SYSTEM.

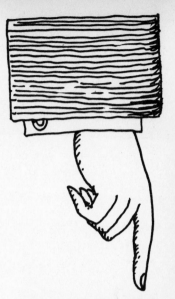

THIS WAS ANOTHER HINT TO EINSTEIN THAT GRAVITY IS A PROPERTY OF SPACE, RATHER THAN OBJECTS.

41

· CHAPTER 5 ·
OTHER ORBITS

So far we've seen only circular orbits: a satellite is projected horizontally with just enough speed so that it falls away from straight-line motion to match the curvature of a circle. But what would happen if we projected it with a different speed, or at another angle?

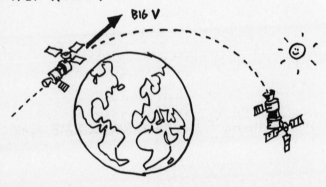

BIG V

ONE WAY TO WORK OUT THE ORBIT IS WITH A TIME-HONORED MATHEMATICAL TECHNIQUE KNOWN AS "BRUTE FORCE."

ALSO KNOWN AS "UGLY MATH."

M   m

42

THE BRUTE-FORCE METHOD
STARTS WITH THE GRAVITATIONAL
FORMULA

$$F = G\frac{Mm}{r^2}.$$

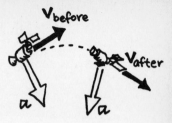

(M = MASS OF EARTH; m = MASS
OF SATELLITE, r = DISTANCE
BETWEEN THEM, G = CONSTANT.)
THIS FORMULA GIVES THE FORCE
ON THE SATELLITE, SO WE CAN
COMPUTE ITS ACCELERATION BY
NEWTON'S SECOND LAW

$$a = F/m.$$ THEN WE CAN
COMPUTE HOW MUCH ITS VELOCITY
CHANGES, OWING TO THIS ACCELERATION.

BUT ALAS — AFTER IT HAS MOVED A LITTLE, r IS
DIFFERENT, SO THE GRAVITATIONAL FORCE ON THE
BODY HAS CHANGED! SO WE NEED TO RE-CALCULATE
THE ACCELERATION AND NEW VELOCITY FOR THE NEXT
FEW MOMENTS... AND THEN RECALCULATE AGAIN...
AND AGAIN... AND AGAIN... AND AGAIN... THOUSANDS OF
TIMES !!!

AT EACH STEP, COMPUTE:
NEW FORCE
NEW ACCELERATION
NEW VELOCITY
NEW POSITION
NEW FORCE
NEW ACCELERATION

ETC.!

(INCIDENTALLY, THIS STEP-BY-STEP PROCEDURE IS CALLED "NUMERICALLY INTEGRATING A DIFFERENTIAL EQUATION.")

"UGLY MATH" IS MUCH MORE DESCRIPTIVE...

IF THERE ARE ONLY TWO BODIES PRESENT, CALCULUS ALLOWS US TO DERIVE FORMULAS FOR THESE ORBITS. WE FIND THAT THE ONLY POSSIBLE ORBITS IN NEWTON'S GRAVITY ARE CIRCLES, ELLIPSES, PARABOLAS, AND HYPERBOLAS.

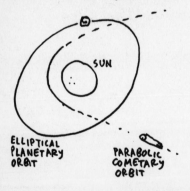

ELLIPTICAL PLANETARY ORBIT

SUN

PARABOLIC COMETARY ORBIT

BUT WHEN THERE ARE MORE THAN TWO BODIES, BRUTE FORCE — AND THE COMPUTER — ARE OUR ONLY HOPE! FOR EXAMPLE, THE MOON FOLLOWS A CORKSCREW PATH AROUND THE SUN!

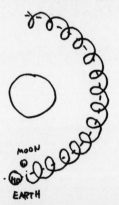

MOON

EARTH

FORTUNATELY, THE SUN IS SO MASSIVE THAT ITS GRAVITY DOMINATES THE SOLAR SYSTEM, AND PLANETARY ORBITS ARE NEARLY EXACT ELLIPSES.

THE FIRST TO SHOW ELLIPTICAL ORBITS WAS **KEPLER** (1571-1630), WHO PROVED THAT THE ORBIT OF MARS WAS AN ELLIPSE. LATER, NEWTON SHOWED HOW ELLIPTICAL ORBITS RESULT FROM AN INVERSE-SQUARE LAW OF FORCE.

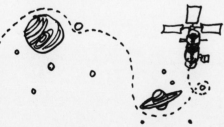

BUT ELLIPSES ARE ONLY APPROXIMATE, AND BRUTE-FORCE MATH IS WHAT WE USE TO SEND OUR SPACE PROBES TO THE PLANETS.

THE EQUATIONS ARE SIMPLE. THEY DESCRIBE THE GENERAL **KIND** OF MOTION, BUT THE ACTUAL MOTION DEPENDS ON THE INITIAL POSITIONS AND VELOCITIES OF ALL THE BODIES. THE SOLAR SYSTEM IS GOVERNED BY $F = G\frac{Mm}{r^2}$ AND $F = ma$, BUT TO LAUNCH THAT SPACE PROBE, WE MUST DO AN IMMENSE CALCULATION.

WE'RE EXPERIENCING A SLIGHT COMPUTER ERROR HERE...

SORRY

MUCH OF PHYSICS IS LIKE THIS: FIND THE GENERAL EQUATIONS AND SOLVE THEM FOR THE SPECIFIC CASE AT HAND. IS IT POSSIBLE, WE WONDER, TO DESCRIBE ALL THE PHYSICS OF THE UNIVERSE WITH A SMALL LIST OF EQUATIONS STARTING FROM THE INITIAL CONDITIONS OF THE **BIG BANG** ?

WHO KNOWS?

·CHAPTER 6·
NEWTON'S THIRD LAW

SO FAR, WE HAVE LOOKED AT NEWTON'S FIRST TWO LAWS: NOW LET'S LOOK AT HIS THIRD LAW. IT IS:

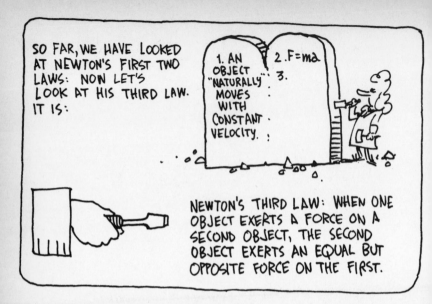

1. AN OBJECT "NATURALLY" MOVES WITH CONSTANT VELOCITY.

2. F=ma

3.

NEWTON'S THIRD LAW: WHEN ONE OBJECT EXERTS A FORCE ON A SECOND OBJECT, THE SECOND OBJECT EXERTS AN EQUAL BUT OPPOSITE FORCE ON THE FIRST.

IN OTHER WORDS,

ACTION EQUALS REACTION.

FOR EXAMPLE, WHEN I PUSH ON A WALL, THE WALL PUSHES BACK WITH EQUAL FORCE. THE EARTH'S GRAVITATIONAL PULL ON THE MOON EQUALS THE MOON'S PULL ON THE EARTH.

THE EARTH'S PULL ON THE MOON KEEPS THE MOON IN A (NEARLY) CIRCULAR ORBIT. BUT WHAT ABOUT THE MOON'S PULL ON THE EARTH?

FORCE ON MOON PULLS IT AWAY FROM STRAIGHT-LINE MOTION

IN FACT, THE MOON PULLING BACK WITH EQUAL FORCE DOES CAUSE THE EARTH TO EXECUTE A SMALL ORBIT! THE EARTH MOVES LESS THAN THE MOON—ACCELERATES LESS— BECAUSE IT IS MUCH MORE MASSIVE.

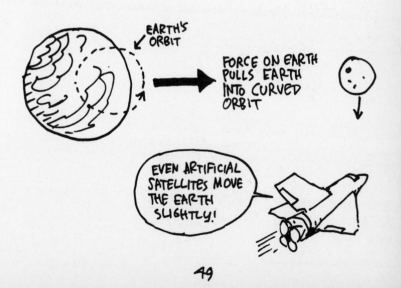

EARTH'S ORBIT

FORCE ON EARTH PULLS EARTH INTO CURVED ORBIT

EVEN ARTIFICIAL SATELLITES MOVE THE EARTH SLIGHTLY!

49

HERE IS A BOOK ON A TABLE. WHAT IS THE FORCE OPPOSITE TO THE BOOK'S WEIGHT **W**? **NOT** THE SUPPORT FORCE FROM THE TABLE!

THE SECOND BODY CAUSING THE FORCE **W** ON THE BOOK IS — **The EARTH!** THE EARTH PULLS THE BOOK WITH FORCE **W**, SO THE BOOK PULLS UP ON THE ENTIRE EARTH WITH FORCE **W**!

W

EARTH

BUT DOESN'T THE TABLE PUSH UP ON THE BOOK? YES, IN THIS CASE. THE BOOK IS NOT ACCELERATING, SO, BY NEWTON'S SECOND LAW, THE TOTAL FORCE ON IT IS ZERO. SINCE THE EARTH PULLS DOWN ON THE BOOK, SOMETHING ELSE MUST BE PUSHING IT UP—NAMELY THE TABLE, AND **F = W**. BUT THIS IS A SPECIAL CASE! IF THE TABLE WASN'T STRONG ENOUGH TO SUPPORT THE BOOK, THE UP-PUSH WOULD BE LESS THAN **W**, AND THE BOOK WOULD BREAK THE TABLE AND FALL!

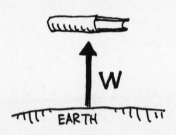

F

W

FORCES ON BOOK

$$F = W$$

F

W

$$F < W$$

HEAVY!

AND ANOTHER EXAMPLE. HOW CAN A HORSE PULL A CART, IF THE CART PULLS BACK WITH AN EQUAL FORCE?? TO ANALYZE THIS, WE HAVE TO LOOK AT EACH OBJECT ALONE AND THE FORCES ACTING ON IT.

WHAT FORCES ACT ON THE CART? THE HORSE PULLS IT FORWARD, AND THERE IS A BACKWARD FORCE FROM THE GROUND: **FRICTION.** IF THE HORSE'S PULL EXCEEDS THE FRICTION, THE CART WILL ACCELERATE.

NOW THE HORSE: THE CART PULLS IT BACKWARD, BY NEWTON'S THIRD LAW. WHAT PUSHES THE HORSE FORWARD? IT'S THE GROUND!! THE HORSE PUSHES BACKWARD ON THE GROUND, SO THE GROUND PUSHES FORWARD WITH AN EQUAL FORCE. IF THE HORSE CAN PUSH BACK AGAINST THE GROUND WITH A FORCE GREATER THAN THE CART'S RESISTING FORCE, THEN THE HORSE WILL ACCELERATE!

51

YET ANOTHER EXAMPLE: A ROCKET ENGINE. THE ROCKET EXERTS A DOWNWARD PUSH ON THE EXHAUST GASES. THE GASES PUSH BACK, BY NEWTON'S THIRD LAW. IF THIS UPWARD THRUST EXCEEDS THE WEIGHT OF THE VEHICLE, UP WE GO!

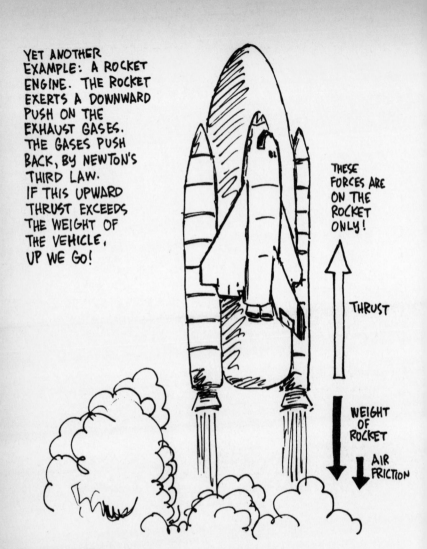

THESE FORCES ARE ON THE ROCKET ONLY!

THRUST

WEIGHT OF ROCKET

AIR FRICTION

NOTE: IT IS NOT NECESSARY FOR THE ESCAPING GASES TO PUSH AGAINST AIR. IN FACT, AIR JUST ACTS AS A FRICTIONAL DRAG ON THE ROCKET.

YES. I NOTICED THAT.

· CHAPTER 7 ·
MORE ABOUT
FORCES

OH, I'VE GOT PLENTY OF NEWTON...

NEWTON'S LAWS CAN BE THOUGHT OF AS DESCRIBING WHAT FORCES DO:

1. WITHOUT ANY FORCES, OBJECTS MAINTAIN CONSTANT VELOCITY.

2. A FORCE PRODUCES AN ACCELERATION PROPORTIONAL TO THE FORCE (AND INVERSELY PROPORTIONAL TO THE MASS.)

3. OBJECTS EXERT EQUAL BUT OPPOSITE FORCES ON EACH OTHER.

FORCE IS A "VECTOR QUANTITY." LIKE VELOCITY AND ACCELERATION, IT HAS NOT ONLY A **MAGNITUDE** BUT ALSO A **DIRECTION.** IN THIS PICTURE, FORCES PULL IN SEVERAL DIFFERENT DIRECTIONS.

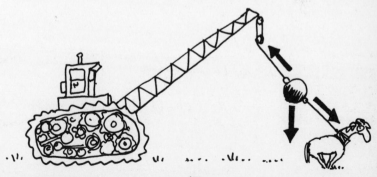

BUT IN THIS CASE, THE SUM
OF ALL THE FORCES, THE
NET FORCE, IS ZERO,
BECAUSE THE MASS IS NOT
ACCELERATING. (NEWTON'S
SECOND LAW AGAIN!)

CONSIDER THE
FORCES ON A
SKIER MOVING
DOWN A HILL
AT CONSTANT
SPEED. THERE ARE
HER WEIGHT, THE
SUPPORT OF
THE GROUND,
AND THE
FORCE OF
FRICTION. BUT
AGAIN, THE
TOTAL FORCE
MUST BE
ZERO.

SUPPORT
FORCE

FRICTION

WEIGHT

DO YOU SEE
WHY THESE
FORCES ADD
TO ZERO?

NOW IMAGINE A TUG OF WAR IN WHICH EACH TEAM PULLS
WITH A FORCE OF 980 NEWTONS. WHAT IS THE TENSION
IN THE ROPE? IS IT 2 × 980 = 1960 NEWTONS?

THE TENSION IS DEFINED AS THE VALUE A SPRING SCALE WOULD
READ IF THE ROPE WERE CUT AND THE SCALE INSERTED:

YOU MIGHT WANT TO
COMPARE THIS SITUATION
TO WEIGHING A 100·kg
MASS WITH A SPRING
SCALE. THE MASS HAS A
WEIGHT OF 980 NEWTONS
(=mg).

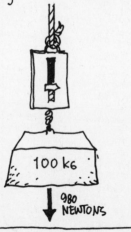

100 kg

980 NEWTONS

THE MASS PULLS DOWN ON THE
SCALE WITH A FORCE OF
980 NEWTONS, SO THE SCALE
PULLS UP ON THE MASS WITH
THE SAME FORCE. THEN THE
SCALE ALSO PULLS DOWN ON
THE CEILING, AND THE CEILING
PULLS BACK WITH 980 NEWTONS
FORCE!

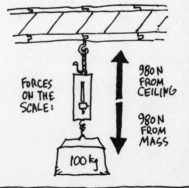

FORCES
ON THE
SCALE:

100 kg

980 N
FROM
CEILING

980 N
FROM
MASS

IN EFFECT, THE STRING TRANSMITS THE FORCE FROM THE MASS THROUGH THE SCALE TO THE CEILING. THE MASS AND THE STRING PULL ON EACH OTHER EQUALLY, BY NEWTON'S THIRD LAW, AND THE TENSION ON THE STRING — THE SCALE READING — IS 980 NEWTONS.

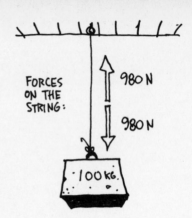

FORCES ON THE STRING:

980 N

980 N

100 KG.

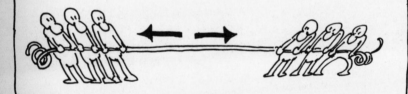

DOES THIS CONVINCE YOU THAT THE TENSION IN THE TUG-OF-WAR ROPE IS **ALSO** 980 NEWTONS? THE ROPE TRANSMITS THE FORCE FROM ONE TEAM TO THE OTHER.

IF YOU TIED ONE END OF THE ROPE TO A POST, AND BOTH TEAMS PULLED TOGETHER, THEN THE TENSION WOULD BE DOUBLED!

UNTIL SOMETHING SNAPS!

ONE FORCE THAT WE ENCOUNTER EVERY DAY IS **FRICTION**. IF YOU PUSH A BOOK ACROSS THE TABLE, YOU FIND THAT FRICTION RESISTS, WHATEVER DIRECTION YOU PUSH. IF YOU START PUSHING GENTLY, YOU'LL FIND THAT THE FRICTION FORCE IS VARIABLE.

IT RESISTS TO A POINT, AND THEN BREAKS FREE!

CAN YOU FEEL THAT FRICTION DECREASES SLIGHTLY AS THE BOOK STARTS TO MOVE? WE SAY THAT THE **STATIC** FRICTION, WHEN THE SURFACES ARE STATIONARY, VARIES UP TO A MAXIMUM VALUE. THE **KINETIC** FRICTION, WHEN THEY ARE MOVING, IS LESS THAN THE MAXIMUM STATIC FRICTION. THAT'S WHY A SKIDDING CAR TAKES LONGER TO STOP THAN ONE WHOSE WHEELS ARE ROLLING.

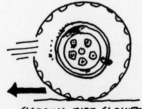

SKIDDING TIRE SLOWED BY KINETIC FRICTION

ROTATING TIRE'S POINT OF CONTACT IS MOMENTARILY STATIONARY (!), SO THE TIRE IS SLOWED BY STATIC FRICTION.

ANOTHER EXAMPLE OF FRICTION IS AIR FRICTION.

YOU CAN FEEL IT BY STICKING YOUR HAND OUT YOUR CAR WINDOW!

AN EXCITING WAY TO EXPERIENCE AIR FRICTION IS TO GO SKYDIVING. WHEN YOU FIRST JUMP, THE ONLY FORCE ON YOU IS GRAVITY, AND YOU ACCELERATE AT A RATE OF g.

W

AS YOU PICK UP SPEED, AIR FRICTION INCREASES, AND YOUR ACCELERATION SLOWS.

friction

W

friction

W

EVENTUALLY, AT 100-150 MPH, THE AIR FRICTION EQUALS YOUR WEIGHT, AND YOUR SPEED INCREASES NO FURTHER. WE CALL THIS NATURAL SPEED LIMIT YOUR TERMINAL VELOCITY.

AIR FRICTION ALSO DEPENDS ON THE AREA "FRONTING THE WIND," WHICH IS WHY A PARACHUTE CAN SLOW YOUR TERMINAL VELOCITY TO 25 MPH OR SO.

SOME FORCES ARE FICTITIOUS !!!

RECALL THE ACCELEROMETER BALL WE HUNG FROM RINGO'S ROLL BAR? IT HANGS BACKWARD WHEN HE ACCELERATES. BUT WHY?

THERE ARE ONLY TWO REAL FORCES ON THE BALL: GRAVITY, WHICH PULLS DOWNWARD WITH MAGNITUDE **mg**, AND THE TENSION T ON THE STRING. WHEN RINGO ACCELERATES, THE TOTAL OF THESE TWO MUST POINT FORWARD WITH MAGNITUDE **ma**, BY NEWTON'S SECOND LAW — SO THE STRING MUST HANG AT AN ANGLE.

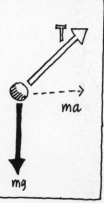

BUT RINGO, IN THE CAR, IMAGINES A STRANGE "ACCELERATION FORCE" PUSHING EVERYTHING BACKWARDS!

BUT THERE IS NOTHING DOING THE PUSHING. THE "FORCE" IS FICTITIOUS, AN EFFECT OF **INERTIA** RESISTING THE CAR'S ACCELERATION.

HA!

ALL THE SIDEWAYS AND BACK-AND-FORTH FORCES YOU FEEL WHILE DRIVING ARE FICTITIOUS, THE RESULT OF YOUR INERTIA RESISTING ACCELERATION.

CAUTION: INERTIA AHEAD

WHEN I SWING A BALL ON A STRING, AROUND MY HEAD, MANY PEOPLE WOULD SAY THAT "CENTRIFUGAL FORCE" KEEPS THE STRING TAUT. BUT THERE IS ACTUALLY NO FORCE PULLING THE BALL OUT: THERE IS NOTHING OUT THERE PULLING THE BALL!

"CENTRIFUGAL FORCE" IS FICTITIOUS! THE ONLY FORCE PULLING ON THE BALL IS THAT OF THE STRING, PULLING TOWARD THE CENTER OF THE CIRCLE — A CENTRIPETAL FORCE. THIS FORCE IS NON-ZERO, SO THE BALL MUST BE ACCELERATING.

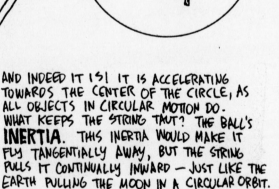

AND INDEED IT IS! IT IS ACCELERATING TOWARDS THE CENTER OF THE CIRCLE, AS ALL OBJECTS IN CIRCULAR MOTION DO. WHAT KEEPS THE STRING TAUT? THE BALL'S INERTIA. THIS INERTIA WOULD MAKE IT FLY TANGENTIALLY AWAY, BUT THE STRING PULLS IT CONTINUALLY INWARD — JUST LIKE THE EARTH PULLING THE MOON IN A CIRCULAR ORBIT.

60

AN AMUSEMENT
PARK OFFERS
SEVERAL FICTITIOUS
FORCES. LOOK AT
THE **ROTOR**:

PEOPLE ENTER A
CYLINDER, WHICH
ROTATES, PRESSING
THEM AGAINST
THE WALL —THEN
THE FLOOR
DROPS AWAY,
LEAVING THEM
PINNED TO
THE WALL!

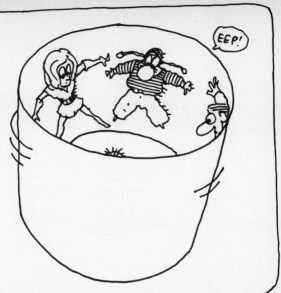

THE PEOPLE INSIDE THE ROTOR FEEL
THE FICTITIOUS **CENTRIFUGAL**
FORCE PUSHING THEM OUTWARD.
BUT OUTSIDE OBSERVERS KNOW
THERE IS ONLY A **CENTRIPETAL**
FORCE FROM THE WALL, PUSHING
THE RIDERS INWARD INTO
CIRCULAR MOTION.

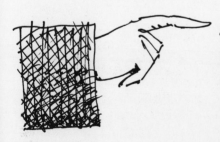

IN AN ACCELERATING
SYSTEM (ROTATING HERE)
FICTITIOUS FORCES
APPEAR. A NON-
ACCELERATING OBSERVER
CAN DESCRIBE THE
MOTION WITH REAL
FORCES AND NEWTON'S
LAWS.

WE SEE SUCH A VARIETY OF FORCES, THAT IT MAY SEEM HOPELESS TO TRY AND ORGANIZE THEM. NEVERTHELESS, PHYSICISTS HAVE BEEN ABLE TO SHOW THAT **ALL** THE KNOWN EFFECTS IN THE UNIVERSE ARE THE RESULT OF THESE

4 BASIC FORCES:

GRAVITY

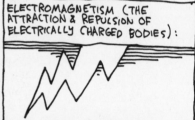
ELECTROMAGNETISM (THE ATTRACTION & REPULSION OF ELECTRICALLY CHARGED BODIES):

THE SUBATOMIC WEAK FORCE:

THE STRONG FORCE HOLDING THE ATOMIC NUCLEUS TOGETHER:

BY THE WAY, THE ONLY ONE OF THE BASIC FORCES YOU'VE EVER FELT IS ELECTROMAGNETISM!! WHEN YOU PUSH THE WALL (AND IT PUSHES BACK), YOU'RE FEELING ELECTRIC REPULSION BETWEEN ATOMS. YOU HAVE NEVER FELT GRAVITY — ONLY THE ELECTRIC FORCES OF THE FLOOR THAT SUPPORT YOU AGAINST GRAVITY.

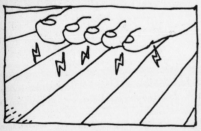

WHEN GRAVITY ALONE ACTS, YOU ARE IN FREE FALL, AND YOU FEEL NO FORCES, REMEMBER?

HELP!

THE "CENTRIFUGAL FORCE" RESEMBLES GRAVITY IN THAT IT PRODUCES ACCELERATIONS INDEPENDENT OF THE MASSES INVOLVED. THAT'S WHY WE CAN SIMULATE GRAVITY WITH THIS BIG CENTRIFUGE USED IN ASTRONAUT TRAINING:

SOMEDAY, WE MAY EVEN BUILD A ROTATING SPACE STATION WITH THE "CENTRIFUGAL FORCE" PROVIDING AN ARTIFICIAL GRAVITY.

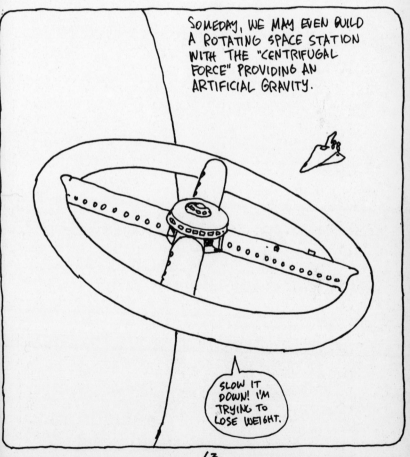

SLOW IT DOWN! I'M TRYING TO LOSE WEIGHT.

· CHAPTER 8 ·
MOMENTUM AND IMPULSE

LET'S GO BACK TO NEWTON'S SECOND LAW, F = ma. SINCE ACCELERATION IS THE RATE OF CHANGE OF VELOCITY OVER TIME, WE CAN RE-WRITE THE EQUATION AS:

FORCE =
mass × (time rate of change of velocity)

NOT QUITE RIGHT, RINGO...

BUT NEWTON BELIEVED THE CORRECT EQUATION SHOULD BE:

FORCE =
time rate of change of (mass × velocity).

YES!

WHICH IS THE SAME ONLY IF MASS DOESN'T CHANGE!

WE CALL THE QUANTITY MASS × VELOCITY THE

MOMENTUM.

THE EQUATION SAYS THAT FORCE DEPENDS ON THE RATE OF CHANGE OF MOMENTUM.

AN OBJECT WITH SMALL MASS AND MODERATE SPEED, LIKE A RUNAWAY BABY CARRIAGE, HAS ONLY MODERATE MOMENTUM. IT DOESN'T REQUIRE MUCH FORCE TO CHANGE ITS MOMENTUM TO ZERO (I.E., TO STOP IT).

A RUNAWAY MACK TRUCK, ON THE OTHER HAND...

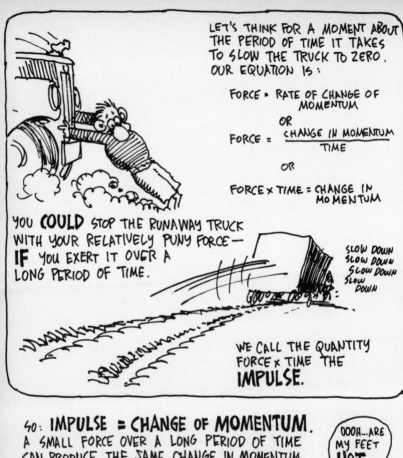

LET'S THINK FOR A MOMENT ABOUT THE PERIOD OF TIME IT TAKES TO SLOW THE TRUCK TO ZERO. OUR EQUATION IS:

$$\text{FORCE} = \text{RATE OF CHANGE OF MOMENTUM}$$

OR

$$\text{FORCE} = \frac{\text{CHANGE IN MOMENTUM}}{\text{TIME}}$$

OR

$$\text{FORCE} \times \text{TIME} = \text{CHANGE IN MOMENTUM}$$

YOU **COULD** STOP THE RUNAWAY TRUCK WITH YOUR RELATIVELY PUNY FORCE— **IF** YOU EXERT IT OVER A LONG PERIOD OF TIME.

SLOW DOWN
SLOW DOWN
SLOW DOWN
SLOW DOWN

WE CALL THE QUANTITY FORCE × TIME THE **IMPULSE.**

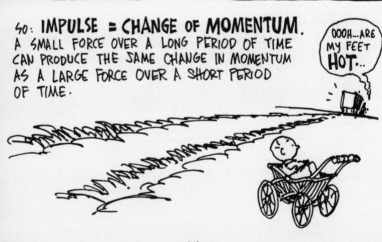

SO: **IMPULSE = CHANGE OF MOMENTUM.** A SMALL FORCE OVER A LONG PERIOD OF TIME CAN PRODUCE THE SAME CHANGE IN MOMENTUM AS A LARGE FORCE OVER A SHORT PERIOD OF TIME.

OOOH...ARE MY FEET **HOT**...

USUALLY WE THINK OF IMPULSE AS A LARGE FORCE ACTING OVER A SHORT TIME, LIKE A BAT HITTING A BALL.

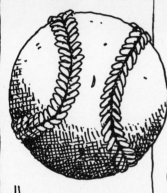

⇓

THE BATTER'S JOB IS TO CHANGE THE BALL'S MOMENTUM FROM MEDIUM IN ONE DIRECTION TO HIGH IN THE OPPOSITE DIRECTION. SINCE THE BAT MEETS THE BALL FOR ONLY A SPLIT SECOND, THE FORCE MUST BE VERY LARGE.

GET ME STEROIDS!

SOMETIMES WE WANT TO MINIMIZE THE FORCE NEEDED TO CHANGE MOMENTUM. A SKYDIVER, EVEN WITH A PARACHUTE, STILL HITS THE GROUND WITH MODERATE MOMENTUM.

WHAT'S THAT BIG BASEBALL?

IF SHE LANDS WITH KNEES LOCKED, HER MOMENTUM DROPS TO ZERO SUDDENLY. SHE FEELS HUGE FORCES IN HER LEGS! OW!

CRAK

BETTER TO DO IT WITH KNEES BENT, ROLLING TO PROLONG THE TIME OF IMPACT, REDUCING THE FORCES.

CONSERVATION OF MOMENTUM

LET'S LOOK FOR A MINUTE AT COLLISIONS AND EXPLOSIONS. BY THIS WE MEAN ANY SITUATION WHERE THINGS ARE COMING TOGETHER OR FLYING APART.

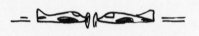

COLLISION ABOUT TO HAPPEN

EXPLOSION ABOUT TO HAPPEN

FOR EXAMPLE, CONSIDER SHOOTING A GUN. THIS IS AN EXPLOSION, IN THE GENERAL SENSE THAT THE BULLET GOES ONE WAY AND THE GUN RECOILS THE OTHER. SUPPOSE, FOR THE SAKE OF SIMPLIFYING THE ARGUMENT, THAT THE BULLET IS EJECTED BY MEANS OF A SPRING:

BIG m
SMALL v

SMALL m
BIG v

WHEN THE SPRING IS RELEASED, IT EXERTS A FORCE ON THE BULLET. BY NEWTON'S THIRD LAW, THE BULLET EXERTS AN EQUAL BUT OPPOSITE FORCE ON THE SPRING/GUN SYSTEM. THESE FORCES PRODUCE EQUAL BUT OPPOSITE CHANGES IN MOMENTUM. SINCE THE GUN IS MORE MASSIVE THAN THE BULLET, IT RECOILS AT A VELOCITY MUCH SMALLER THAN THE BULLET'S VELOCITY.

IN THIS CASE, THERE WAS NO NET CHANGE IN MOMENTUM. IF THE GUN AND BULLET WERE INITIALLY AT REST, THE MOMENTUM WAS ZERO AT FIRST. SINCE THE SPRING RELEASE DID NOT CHANGE THE TOTAL MOMENTUM, THE FINAL MOMENTUM IS ALSO ZERO: THE BULLET AND GUN HAVE EQUAL AND OPPOSITE MOMENTUM.

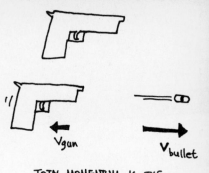

V_{gun}

V_{bullet}

TOTAL MOMENTUM IS THE SAME BEFORE AND AFTER FIRING

AFTER A LITTLE DISCUSSION, SCIENTISTS FOUND A PROPERLY SCIENTIFIC WAY TO SAY, "MOMENTUM DOESN'T CHANGE."

MOMENTUM IS CONSERVED.

CONSERVATION OF MOMENTUM IS A CONSEQUENCE OF NEWTON'S THIRD LAW. CONSIDER A FLYING PROJECTILE THAT EXPLODES INTO SEVERAL PIECES, LIKE THIS MULTIPLE-WARHEAD MISSILE:

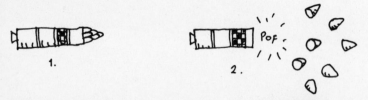

1.

2.

THE FORCES BETWEEN THE PIECES WE CALL **INTERNAL** FORCES. (THERE MAY ALSO BE EXTERNAL FORCES, SUCH AS GRAVITY.) BY NEWTON'S THIRD LAW, THE INTERNAL FORCES ACT IN EQUAL BUT OPPOSITE PAIRS. ANY FORCE ON ONE PIECE IS OFFSET BY AN EQUAL AND OPPOSITE FORCE ON ANOTHER PIECE.

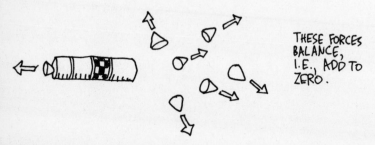

THESE FORCES BALANCE, I.E., ADD TO ZERO.

THEREFORE, THE INTERNAL FORCES CAN PRODUCE NO NET CHANGE IN MOMENTUM. EXPLOSIONS CONSERVE MOMENTUM.

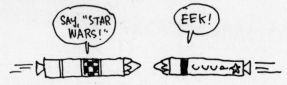

THE SAME ARGUMENT HOLDS FOR COLLISIONS, WHICH MIGHT BE CALLED EXPLOSIONS IN REVERSE.

WE USED A ROCKET TO ILLUSTRATE NEWTON'S THIRD LAW, AND IT ALSO ILLUSTRATES CONSERVATION OF MOMENTUM. TO ACCELERATE IN SPACE, YOU MUST EJECT SOMETHING THE OTHER WAY — NAMELY, THE EXHAUST GASES. IF I'M SPACEWALKING, AND MY PROPELLANT SYSTEMS FAIL, HOW CAN I GET BACK? BY THROWING SOMETHING, SAY ONE OF MY TOOLS, IN THE OPPOSITE DIRECTION.

WILL THE FAN BLOWING ON THE SAIL MOVE THIS SAILBOAT? NO! (NOT UNLESS SOME OF THE WIND FROM THE FAN MISSES THE SAIL, OR BOUNCES OFF IT OUT THE OTHER WAY.)

TSK!

SOMETHING MUST MOVE AWAY FROM THE SAILBOAT ONE WAY FOR IT TO BE PUSHED THE OTHER WAY.

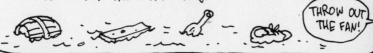

THROW OUT THE FAN!

MOMENTUM CONSERVATION WAS FIRST DERIVED FROM NEWTON'S THIRD LAW. BUT WE HAVE COME TO BELIEVE THAT CONSERVATION OF MOMENTUM IS THE MORE FUNDAMENTAL LAW, AND NEWTON'S LAW IS A CONSEQUENCE OF IT. IN ANY CLOSED SYSTEM, BY DEFINITION, THERE ARE NO EXTERNAL FORCES, SO MOMENTUM IS CONSERVED.

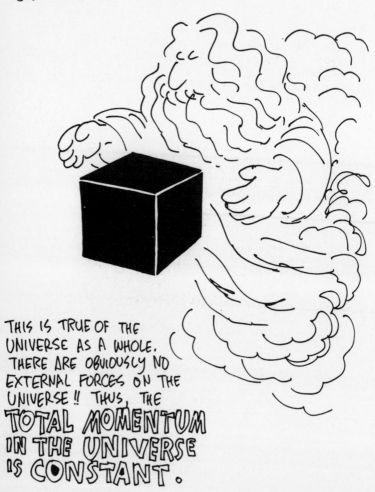

THIS IS TRUE OF THE UNIVERSE AS A WHOLE. THERE ARE OBVIOUSLY NO EXTERNAL FORCES ON THE UNIVERSE!! THUS, THE **TOTAL MOMENTUM IN THE UNIVERSE IS CONSTANT.**

·CHAPTER 9·
ENERGY

ISAAC NEWTON ALMOST
SINGLE-HANDEDLY INVENTED
THE SCIENCE OF MECHANICS,
BUT THERE IS ONE CONCEPT
HE MISSED: **ENERGY**.

ENERGY COMES IN MANY FORMS, BUT THE BASIC DEFINITION IS IN TERMS OF

WORK.

NO WONDER I AVOIDED THE LOATHSOME IDEA!

WE ALL HAVE A CONCEPT OF WORK, BUT IN PHYSICS, THE DEFINITION IS VERY PRECISE: WE SAY THAT WORK IS DONE WHEN A FORCE **F** MOVES A BODY THROUGH A DISTANCE **d**. WORK IS DEFINED AS **FORCE TIMES DISTANCE.**

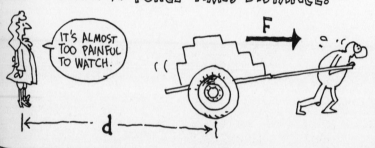

IT'S ALMOST TOO PAINFUL TO WATCH.

F

d

$W = F \times d$

IN THIS DEFINITION, ONLY THE FORCE IN THE DIRECTION OF MOTION COUNTS. IF I PULL A WAGON AT AN ANGLE, ONLY THE HORIZONTAL PART OF THE PULL DOES ANY WORK.

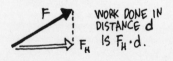

F

F_H

WORK DONE IN DISTANCE **d** IS $F_H \cdot d$.

74

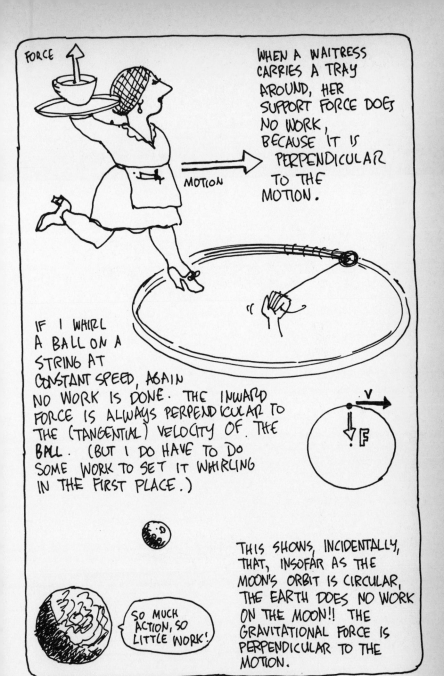

FORCE

WHEN A WAITRESS CARRIES A TRAY AROUND, HER SUPPORT FORCE DOES NO WORK, BECAUSE IT IS PERPENDICULAR TO THE MOTION.

MOTION

IF I WHIRL A BALL ON A STRING AT CONSTANT SPEED, AGAIN NO WORK IS DONE. THE INWARD FORCE IS ALWAYS PERPENDICULAR TO THE (TANGENTIAL) VELOCITY OF THE BALL. (BUT I DO HAVE TO DO SOME WORK TO SET IT WHIRLING IN THE FIRST PLACE.)

V

F

SO MUCH ACTION, SO LITTLE WORK!

THIS SHOWS, INCIDENTALLY, THAT, INSOFAR AS THE MOON'S ORBIT IS CIRCULAR, THE EARTH DOES NO WORK ON THE MOON!! THE GRAVITATIONAL FORCE IS PERPENDICULAR TO THE MOTION.

ENERGY

IS DEFINED AS THE CAPACITY TO DO WORK. THE RELEASE OF ENERGY DOES WORK — AND DOING WORK ON SOMETHING ADDS ENERGY TO IT. SO — ENERGY AND WORK ARE ACTUALLY **EQUIVALENT CONCEPTS**, AND WE WRITE:

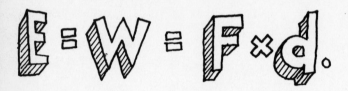

$$E = W = F \times d.$$

IN THE ENGLISH SYSTEM, THE UNIT OF ENERGY IS THE **FOOT·POUND** (FEET × POUNDS), AND IN THE METRIC SYSTEM IT'S THE **NEWTON·METER**, WHICH IS ALSO CALLED THE **JOULE**.

YOU TELL 'EM ABOUT THE JOULE — I'M GOING TO TRY POUNDING FEET...

SO: ONE **JOULE** = THE ABILITY TO EXERT A FORCE OF ONE **NEWTON** OVER A DISTANCE OF ONE **METER**.

OO!

$F = 1$ NEWTON

10 20 30 40 50 60 70 80 90 100

KINETIC & POTENTIAL ENERGY

SUPPOSE I THROW A BALL. I DO WORK GETTING THE BALL MOVING: I EXERT A FORCE **F** OVER A DISTANCE **d**. THE BALL THEN HAS ACQUIRED SOME ENERGY, THE ENERGY OF MOTION, OR **KINETIC** ENERGY. A SIMPLE MATHEMATICAL DERIVATION*SHOWS THAT

$$K.E. = \frac{1}{2}mv^2$$

HERE m IS THE BALL'S MASS, AND v IS ITS VELOCITY.

ON THE OTHER HAND, SUPPOSE I LIFT RINGO TO A HEIGHT **h**. AS I EXERT A FORCE **W** = RINGO'S WEIGHT OVER A DISTANCE **h**, I DO WORK $W \cdot h = mgh$. RINGO ISN'T MOVING AT THE END, BUT HE STILL HAS AN ADDED ENERGY OF mgh, JUST BECAUSE OF WHERE HE IS IN THE EARTH'S GRAVITATIONAL FIELD. THIS ENERGY IS CALLED HIS **POTENTIAL** ENERGY.

$$P.E. = mgh.$$

* ASSUME F CONSTANT. $F = ma$, SO $KE = F \cdot d = mad$. BUT $d = \frac{1}{2}at^2$, SO $KE = \frac{1}{2}m(at)^2$. BUT $v = at$, SO $KE = \frac{1}{2}mv^2$.

POTENTIAL ENERGY IS POTENTIAL BECAUSE IT CAN BE GOTTEN BACK AS "REAL" KINETIC ENERGY. ALL I HAVE TO DO IS LET RINGO FALL!

OH, COME ON!

AS HE FALLS FASTER AND FASTER, HIS POTENTIAL ENERGY IS GRADUALLY CONVERTED INTO KINETIC ENERGY. AT THE BOTTOM, JUST BEFORE IMPACT, HIS POTENTIAL ENERGY IS ZERO, AND HIS ORIGINAL POTENTIAL ENERGY HAS BECOME ENTIRELY KINETIC. THAT IS,

$$\frac{1}{2}mv^2 = mgh$$

SIGH

FROM THIS YOU CAN SOLVE FOR **v**, HIS VELOCITY UPON IMPACT. $v = \sqrt{2gh}$.

DO YOU THINK LUCY HAS A SADISTIC STREAK?

THIS LAST EQUALITY $\frac{1}{2}mv^2 = mgh$ IS AN EXAMPLE OF

☆ CONSERVATION OF ENERGY. ☆

AS THE CONCEPT OF ENERGY WAS DEVELOPED, PHYSICISTS GRADUALLY REALIZED THAT ENERGY, LIKE MOMENTUM, IS CONSERVED.

A UNIVERSAL LAW!

(THE CONFUSING PART WAS THAT ENERGY, UNLIKE MOMENTUM, APPEARS IN MANY DISGUISES, SUCH AS HEAT, AS WE'LL SEE.)

HERE'S AN APPLICATION OF ENERGY CONSERVATION. IF V_0 IS THE INITIAL SPEED OF THIS ROLLER COASTER, WE CAN COMPUTE ITS SPEED AT ANY POINT, JUST FROM KNOWING HOW FAR IT HAS DESCENDED! LET h BE THE DISTANCE DESCENDED, AND V_F ITS FINAL VELOCITY. THEN:

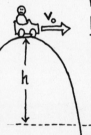

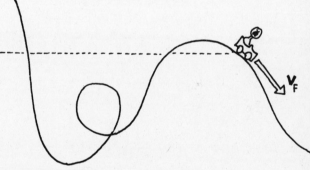

INITIAL ENERGY $= \frac{1}{2}mv_0^2 + mgh$

FINAL ENERGY $= \frac{1}{2}mv_F^2$

THESE ARE EQUAL, BY CONSERVATION OF ENERGY.

$\frac{1}{2}mv_F^2 = \frac{1}{2}mv_0^2 + mgh$, SO

$$V_F = \sqrt{V_0^2 + 2gh}$$

CONSERVATION OF ENERGY TELLS US THAT THE TOTAL ENERGY OF THE SYSTEM DOES NOT CHANGE — BUT THE ENERGY MAY BE CONVERTED INTO OTHER FORMS. WHAT HAPPENS TO RINGO'S ENERGY WHEN HE HITS THE FLOOR? NOW BOTH THE KINETIC AND POTENTIAL ENERGIES ARE GONE!

SO IS MY ENTHUSIASM...

WHERE DID THEY GO?

LET'S LOOK AT THE IMPACT ITSELF. SOME OF THE ENERGY IS CONVERTED INTO **SOUND**. SOME GOES INTO DISTORTING THE FLOOR — AND DISTORTING RINGO, FOR THAT MATTER. AND SOME, EVEN MOST, GOES INTO **HEAT**. RINGO AND THE FLOOR ARE BOTH A LITTLE WARMER AFTER THE COLLISION. THE IMPACT JIGGLES THEIR MOLECULES — AND HEAT IS NOTHING BUT THE KINETIC ENERGY OF BILLIONS OF MOLECULES !!!

CRACK

FLOOR MOVES

HEAT RISES

SOUND ENERGY

SPLAT

VARIOUS FORMS OF ENERGY
CHANGE INTO EACH OTHER
CONSTANTLY. IN THE SCIENCE
OF **THERMODYNAMICS**
WE LEARN THAT IT IS EASY
TO CONVERT KINETIC ENERGY
INTO HEAT, BUT MUCH HARDER
TO CONVERT HEAT INTO
KINETIC ENERGY.

RUB
RUB
CONVERTING
KINETIC ENERGY
INTO HEAT

DEVICE FOR CONVERTING
HEAT INTO MOVEMENT

CAR ENGINES CONVERT
HEAT INTO MOVEMENT,
BUT NOT EFFICIENTLY.
YOUR CAR NEEDS A
COOLING SYSTEM, AND
MUCH HEAT ESCAPES.

RESULT:
HEAT
POLLUTION!

BUT ENERGY IS ALWAYS CONSERVED — IN OTHER WORDS:

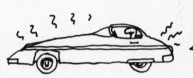

HEAT
GOING
IN
= {
WORK PRODUCED
+
HEAT COMING OUT
}

PHEW!
HOT
LEMONADE!

WHEN I LIFT RINGO, I PUT ENERGY INTO HIM. WHERE DID THAT ENERGY COME FROM?

IT'S MUSCULAR ENERGY, WHICH IN TURN IS RELEASED CHEMICAL ENERGY CAUSED BY FOOD OXIDIZING IN MY BODY.

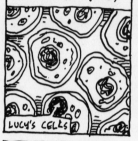

LUCY'S CELLS

CHEMICAL ENERGY IS A FORM OF POTENTIAL ENERGY, OWING TO THE POSITIONS OF ELECTRONS IN MOLECULES' ELECTRICAL FIELDS.

THE CHEMICAL ENERGY CAME FROM A PLANT THAT I ATE. (I'M A VEGETARIAN.)

THE PLANT CONVERTED THE RADIANT ENERGY OF SUNLIGHT INTO CHEMICAL ENERGY VIA PHOTOSYNTHESIS.

THE SUNLIGHT CAME FROM NUCLEAR FUSION IN THE SUN.

AND THE SUN'S HYDROGEN NUCLEI WERE CREATED FROM THE ENERGY OF THE CREATION EVENT OF THE UNIVERSE, THE

BIG BANG.

EVEN THE ENERGY MOVING THE CARTOONIST'S PEN CAN BE TRACED BACK IN THIS WAY TO THE BIG BANG!!

·CHAPTER 10·
COLLISIONS

COLLISIONS PROVIDE GOOD ILLUSTRATIONS OF THE CONSERVATION OF MOMENTUM AND ENERGY. LET'S START BY LETTING SOME THINGS COLLIDE WITH THE GROUND. I'LL DROP SOME BALLS MADE OF VARIOUS MATERIALS, AND SEE HOW HIGH THEY BOUNCE. AS YOU CAN SEE, SOME BOUNCE HIGHER THAN OTHERS.

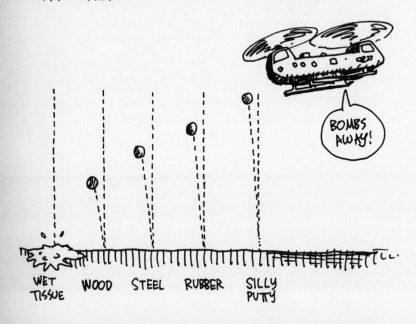

BOMBS AWAY!

WET TISSUE WOOD STEEL RUBBER SILLY PUTTY

IF A BALL BOUNCES BACK TO THE ORIGINAL HEIGHT, WE SAY IT IS

TOTALLY ELASTIC.

STRETCHY!

COLLISIONS RANGE FROM
TOTALLY ELASTIC TO
TOTALLY INELASTIC. IN
A TOTALLY INELASTIC
COLLISION, THE BALL
DOESN'T BOUNCE BACK
AT ALL, LIKE THE
WAD OF WET TISSUE
OR A BLOB OF PUTTY.

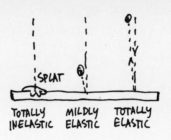

TOTALLY | MILDLY | TOTALLY
INELASTIC | ELASTIC | ELASTIC

IN A TOTALLY ELASTIC COLLISION, NO KINETIC ENERGY IS LOST
AS HEAT ON IMPACT. THE UPWARD SPEED AFTER THE BOUNCE
IS THE SAME AS THE DOWNWARD SPEED JUST BEFORE. IN A

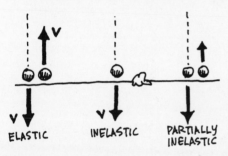

ELASTIC | INELASTIC | PARTIALLY
INELASTIC

TOTALLY INELASTIC
COLLISION, THE BALL STICKS
UPON IMPACT, LOSING ALL
ITS KINETIC ENERGY...
AND IN A PARTIALLY
INELASTIC COLLISION,
SOME OF THE BALL'S K.E.
IS LOST, AND ON
SUCCESSIVE BOUNCES,
THE BALL "RUNS DOWN."

YOU MIGHT THINK THAT
NO REAL OBJECTS ARE
ABSOLUTELY ELASTIC,
BUT COLLISIONS BETWEEN
ATOMS CAN BE. SINCE
HEAT IS THE RANDOM
KINETIC ENERGY OF MANY
ATOMS, HEAT DOES NOT
EXIST AT THE LEVEL
OF ONE OR TWO ATOMS!

AT THIS
LEVEL,
EVEN HELL
IS COOL!

HERE IS A TOTALLY INELASTIC COLLISION. A LOADED
FREIGHT CAR, MASS 100,000 kg, ROLLS AT 3 m/sec
INTO A STATIONARY CAR OF MASS 50,000 kg. WHEN
THEY HIT, THE COUPLER ENGAGES. (THIS MAKES IT
INELASTIC.) THEN WHAT HAPPENS?

100,000 kg
3 m/sec

SOLUTION: WE WANT TO FIND THE VELOCITY OF THE
COUPLED CARS. CALL IT **V**. THEN:

INITIAL MOMENTUM = 100,000 kg × 3 m/sec

FINAL MOMENTUM = 150,000 kg × V

SINCE MOMENTUM IS CONSERVED, THESE TWO ARE EQUAL:

$$150,000 \text{ kg} \cdot V = 300,000 \text{ M} \cdot \text{kg/sec.}$$

SO:

$$V = 2 \text{ M/sec.}$$

OH, I'VE
BEEN WORKING
ON MO·
MENT·UM...

HERE'S A 2-DIMENSIONAL EXAMPLE: AN 80-KG FOOTBALL PLAYER GOING NORTH AT 3 M/S IS TACKLED BY A 100-KG PLAYER GOING EAST AT 2 M/SEC. AFTER THE IMPACT, WHICH WAY ARE THEY GOING, AND HOW FAST?

LET'S VIEW IT FROM ABOVE:

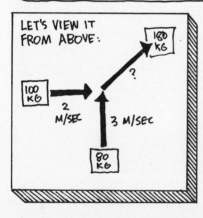

EASTWARD MOMENTUM $= 200 \frac{M \cdot KG}{SEC}$

NORTHWARD MOMENTUM $= 240 \frac{M \cdot KG}{SEC}$

TOTAL MASS $= 180$ kg

SO:

FINAL EAST-WARD VELOCITY $= \frac{200}{180} = 1.1$ M/SEC

FINAL NORTH-WARD VELOCITY $= \frac{240}{180} = 1.33$ M/SEC

THE FINAL DIRECTION IS THE VECTOR SUM:

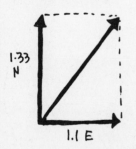

THE LENGTH OF THIS ARROW IS THE FINAL SPEED:

$$V_F = \sqrt{(1.1)^2 + (1.33)^2}$$

$$= 1.7 \text{ M/SEC.}$$

THIS "EXECUTIVE TOY" OF
HANGING BALLS ILLUSTRATES
AN ELASTIC COLLISION:

WHAT WON'T
EXECUTIVES
DO NEXT?

I LET ONE BALL FALL...

...AND ONE BALL FLIES OFF!

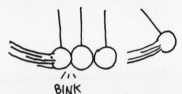

BINK

KINETIC ENERGY IS CONSERVED,
SO THE COLLISION IS ELASTIC.

WHY DON'T TWO BALLS FLY OUT WITH HALF THE SPEED? THAT
WOULD CONSERVE MOMENTUM, AS $mv = \frac{1}{2}mv + \frac{1}{2}mv$.

BUT IT WOULDN'T
CONSERVE
KINETIC ENERGY. THE
INCOMING BALL HAS
K.E. $= \frac{1}{2}mv^2$. TWO
BALLS WITH HALF THE
SPEED HAVE
K.E. $= \frac{1}{2}m(\frac{1}{2}v)^2 + \frac{1}{2}m(\frac{1}{2}v)^2$

$= \frac{1}{4}mv^2$

$\neq \frac{1}{2}mv^2$

ELASTIC
COLLISIONS
CONSERVE
MOMENTUM
AND
KINETIC
ENERGY.

EXECUTIVES
AGREE!

WITH JUST TWO BALLS, WE CAN SEE AN ELASTIC COLLISION BETWEEN TWO EQUAL MASSES:

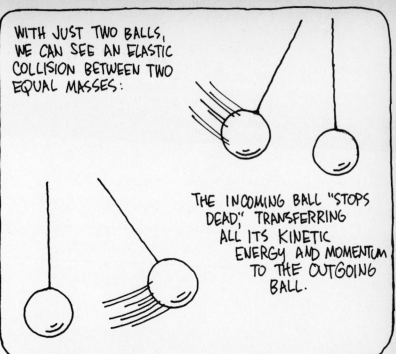

THE INCOMING BALL "STOPS DEAD," TRANSFERRING ALL ITS KINETIC ENERGY AND MOMENTUM TO THE OUTGOING BALL.

YOU SEE THE SAME SITUATION, APPROXIMATELY, IN THE HEAD-ON COLLISION OF BILLIARD BALLS — BUT WITH BILLIARD BALLS, SOME OF THE KINETIC ENERGY IS IN THE BALL'S **ROTATION,** WHICH BRINGS US TO THE NEXT SECTION...

WISH YOU COULD PLAY THIS IN OUTER SPACE...

CHAPTER 11

ROTATION

WE ARE ALL AWARE THAT A MASSIVE OBJECT, LIKE THIS "WHEEL OF FORTUNE," HAS **ROTATIONAL INERTIA.** IT'S HARD TO START MOVING, AND ONCE IT'S GOING, IT RUNS A LONG TIME BEFORE FRICTION BRINGS IT TO A HALT. JUST AS ORDINARY INERTIA RESISTS ACCELERATIONS, ROTATIONAL INERTIA RESISTS ROTATIONAL ACCELERATION.

FUPPA FUPPA

SLOW DOWN SLOW DOWN...

THAT THING HAS SPUN THROUGH THREE COMMERCIALS ALREADY...

DID YOU REALIZE THAT ROTATIONAL INERTIA DEPENDS NOT ONLY ON MASS, BUT ALSO ON HOW MASS IS DISTRIBUTED? MASS ON THE OUTSIDE, AWAY FROM THE CENTER, HAS MORE ROTATIONAL INERTIA THAN MASS CLOSER TO THE CENTER!

HIGH ROTATIONAL INERTIA

LOW ROTATIONAL INERTIA

LET'S RACE A "RIM-LOADED" WHEEL AGAINST A MASS-CENTERED WHEEL DOWN AN INCLINED PLANE. THE MASS-CENTERED WHEEL QUICKLY TAKES THE LEAD, BECAUSE IT IS EASIER TO GET ROTATING THAN THE RIM-LOADED WHEEL.

WE SAY THAT ROTATIONAL INERTIA IS THE **ROTATIONAL ANALOG** OF MASS.

91

IF ROTATIONAL INERTIA IS ANALOGOUS TO MASS, WHAT IS THE ROTATIONAL ANALOG OF **FORCE**? HERE RINGO OPENS A MASSIVE DOOR, BY PUSHING AS FAR FROM THE HINGES AS POSSIBLE, AND HIS PUSH IS PERPENDICULAR TO THE DOOR.

TOP VIEW:

HINGE

CAUTION! CONTAINS SECRETS OF THE UNIVERSE...

THE SAME PRINCIPLE APPLIES WHEN YOU USE A WRENCH TO REMOVE A NUT. YOU GRASP THE WRENCH AS FAR OUT AS POSSIBLE AND PUSH OR PULL PERPENDICULAR TO THE WRENCH.

WE CALL $r_\perp$ ("R-PERP"), THE PERPENDICULAR DISTANCE FROM THE PIVOT POINT TO THE LINE OF FORCE, THE

LEVER ARM.

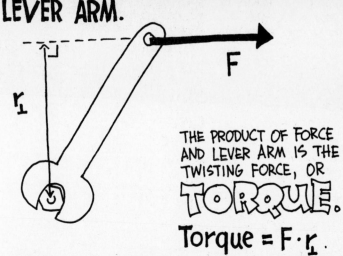

THE PRODUCT OF FORCE AND LEVER ARM IS THE TWISTING FORCE, OR

TORQUE.

Torque = $F \cdot r_\perp$.

TORQUE IS THE ROTATIONAL ANALOG OF FORCE.

· ·

NOTE HOW MAKING F PERPENDICULAR TO THE RADIUS (THE WRENCH) MAXIMIZES $r_\perp$. IN OTHER WORDS, A PERPENDICULAR PUSH IS THE MOST EFFECTIVE PUSH!

$r_\perp$

F

THAT, AND A LONGER WRENCH.

OUR FINAL ROTATIONAL ANALOG IS

ANGULAR MOMENTUM.

BY ANALOGY WITH LINEAR MOMENTUM (MASS TIMES VELOCITY), ANGULAR MOMENTUM IS DEFINED AS

ROTATIONAL INERTIA

✕

ANGULAR VELOCITY.

(ANGULAR VELOCITY IS JUST THE TURNING RATE. IT CAN BE EXPRESSED IN REVOLUTIONS PER SECOND.)

UNLIKE MASS, THE AMOUNT OF ROTATIONAL INERTIA CAN BE CHANGED "IN MID·FLIGHT" BY REARRANGING THE MASS. THIS MAKES ROTATIONAL MOTION MORE COMPLICATED THAN LINEAR MOTION.

TAKE, FOR EXAMPLE, THE CASE OF THE SPINNING ICE SKATER...

94

REMEMBER THAT MOMENTUM IS CONSERVED IN THE ABSENCE OF EXTERNAL FORCES. LIKEWISE, **ANGULAR** MOMENTUM IS CONSERVED IN THE ABSENCE OF EXTERNAL **TORQUES.**

THE SKATER BEGINS SPINNING WITH HER ARMS EXTENDED.

BUT WHEN SHE PULLS IN HER ARMS, HER ROTATIONAL INERTIA GOES DOWN. HER ANGULAR MOMENTUM REMAINS CONSTANT—SO HER ANGULAR VELOCITY INCREASES!

WOW!

IN THIS RESPECT, AN ICE SKATER RESEMBLES A COLLAPSING STAR. THEY BOTH CONSERVE ANGULAR MOMENTUM!

WHEN A ROTATING STAR DIES, IT BEGINS TO COLLAPSE FROM THE FORCE OF ITS OWN GRAVITY.

ITS SPIN INCREASES TO CONSERVE ANGULAR MOMENTUM.

AND IT ENDS UP AS A SUPER-DENSE BLOB OF STUFF, SPINNING MANY TIMES PER SECOND.

TRY TO REMEMBER...

LARGE ROTATIONAL INERTIA × SMALL SPIN RATE
=
SMALL ROTATIONAL INERTIA × LARGE SPIN RATE

ROTATIONAL MOTION HOLDS SOME SURPRISES IN STORE. HERE'S A BICYCLE WHEEL HANGING BY ONE END OF ITS AXLE. NATURALLY, IT FLOPS OVER ON ITS SIDE ...

BUT NOT IF IT'S SPINNING FAST! A SPINNING WHEEL DOESN'T FALL — IT **PRECESSESS.** THAT IS, ITS AXIS ROTATES IN A HORIZONTAL PLANE!

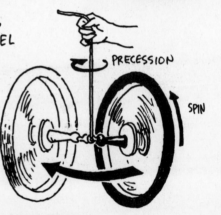

PRECESSION

SPIN

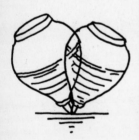

A TOY TOP IS A MORE FAMILIAR EXAMPLE. GRAVITY DOESN'T MAKE IT FALL — IT PRECESSES. AND THE TORQUE ON THE EARTH, CAUSED BY THE MOON'S GRAVITY, MAKES THE EARTH'S AXIS PRECESS ONE REVOLUTION EVERY 26,000 YEARS.

NOW LET'S PUT OUR MECHANICS
KNOWLEDGE TO THE
ULTIMATE TEST:

CHANGING THE CLUTCH IN A '58 EDSEL?

NO... LET'S SEE IF WE CAN UNDERSTAND PRECESSION.... BUT FIRST, AN OBSERVATION ABOUT LINEAR MOTION: SUPPOSE AN OBJECT IS AT REST, AND A FORCE ACTS ON IT. THEN THE OBJECT STARTS TO ACCELERATE IN THE DIRECTION OF THE FORCE.

OBJECT AT REST

A FORCE (GRAVITY) ACTS

INCREASING VELOCITY IS IN THE DIRECTION OF THE FORCE.

Howerver, IF THE OBJECT IS ALREADY MOVING, AND THE FORCE ALWAYS ACTS AT RIGHT ANGLES TO THE MOTION, WE GET **UNIFORM CIRCULAR MOTION.** THE FORCE CURVES THE VELOCITY AROUND, BUT DOES NOT CHANGE THE SPEED.

OBJECT HAS VELOCITY TO BEGIN WITH

DIRECTION CHANGES, BUT NOT SPEED

FORCE ACTS PERPENDICULAR TO MOTION

FORCE CONTINUES PERPENDICULAR TO MOTION

ETC!

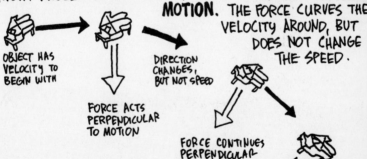

97

SOMETHING SIMILAR
HAPPENS WITH
ROTATION: WHEN THE
WHEEL IS NOT
SPINNING, THE TORQUE
FROM THE WEIGHT
ACCELERATES THE
WHEEL ANGULARLY
AROUND THE TORQUE
AXIS, IN THIS
CASE THE y·AXIS.

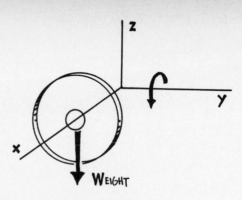

BUT IF THE WHEEL IS
SPINNING, IT ALREADY
HAS ANGULAR MOMENTUM
AROUND THE X·AXIS.
THE TORQUE ADDS
SOME SPIN AROUND
THE y·AXIS,
PERPENDICULAR TO
THE ORIGINAL SPIN.
THE RESULTING SPIN
AXIS IS TURNED A
LITTLE IN THE
$x·y$ PLANE.

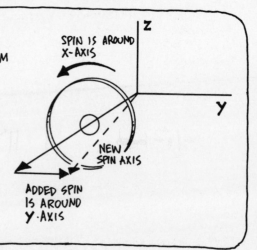

SPIN IS AROUND
X-AXIS

NEW
SPIN AXIS

ADDED SPIN
IS AROUND
y·AXIS

THE TORQUE CONTINUES
TO ACT PERPENDICULAR
TO THE SPIN AXIS, SO
THE PRECESSION
CONTINUES. ANALOGOUSLY
TO THE LINEAR CASE,
THE DIRECTION, BUT NOT
THE SIZE, OF THE SPIN
HAS CHANGED.
CLEAR?

CLEAR
AS A
WHIRLPOOL
IN A
MUD PUDDLE...

THE ARGUMENT ON THE LAST PAGE WAS BASED ON THE CONCEPTS OF TORQUE AND ANGULAR MOMENTUM. BUT THESE CONCEPTS ARE ULTIMATELY BASED ON NEWTON'S SECOND LAW, $F = ma$. LET'S SEE IF WE CAN UNDERSTAND PRECESSION JUST FROM $F = ma$.

WATCH CAREFULLY!

FIRST: THE TORQUE EXERTED BY GRAVITY TENDS TO MAKE THE WHEEL FLOP OVER. SO THERE'S AN OUTWARD FORCE ON THE TOP HALF OF THE WHEEL, AND AN INWARD FORCE ON THE BOTTOM HALF.

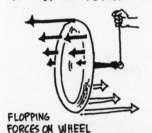

FLOPPING FORCES ON WHEEL

NOW LOOK AT A SMALL PIECE OF THE WHEEL AS IT SPINS. AS IT PASSES THROUGH THE UPPER HALF, IT EXPERIENCES CONTINUAL OUTWARD FORCE.

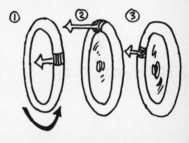

THEREFORE, IT ACCELERATES **OUTWARD**, REACHING MAXIMUM OUTWARD VELOCITY WHEN IT IS AT THE SIDEWAYS POSITION, ABOUT TO ENTER THE WHEEL'S BOTTOM HALF.

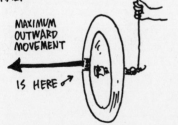

MAXIMUM OUTWARD MOVEMENT

IS HERE

SIMILARLY, EACH PIECE OF THE WHEEL HAS MAXIMUM **INWARD** VELOCITY AT THE "HORIZONTAL-ASCENDING" SPOT.

MAXIMUM INWARD MOVEMENT IS HERE.

SO - AS YOU SEE, THE WHEEL PRECESSES INSTEAD OF FLOPPING!

WELL, I SPENT SO MUCH TIME EXPLAINING PRECESSION TO YOU IN ORDER TO SHOW HOW COMPLICATED THINGS CAN GET, JUST STARTING FROM THAT SIMPLE EQUATION $F = ma$. PHYSICS IS AMAZING THAT WAY.... WHO KNOWS? MAYBE WE **WILL** REDUCE THE PHYSICS OF THE ENTIRE UNIVERSE TO A PAGE FULL OF EQUATIONS !!

·PART TWO·
ELECTRICITY
AND
MAGNETISM

N S

CHAPTER 12
CHARGE

WE NOW TURN FROM MECHANICS TO ELECTRICITY AND MAGNETISM. IN MECHANICS WE USED THE BASIC PROPERTY OF MATTER CALLED **MASS.** IN ELECTRICITY, THE BASIC CONCEPT IS **CHARGE.**

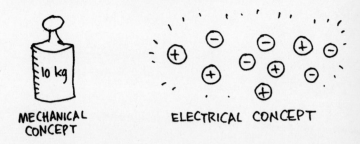

MECHANICAL CONCEPT

ELECTRICAL CONCEPT

NOTICE THAT MECHANICS NEVER TOLD US WHAT MASS "REALLY IS," BUT ONLY HOW IT BEHAVES. IN THE SAME WAY, CLASSICAL E&M TELLS US HOW CHARGE BEHAVES, BUT NOT WHAT IT IS.

IT IS EASY TO PRODUCE A LITTLE CHARGE — JUST RUN A RUBBER COMB THROUGH YOUR HAIR, OR RUB A RUBBER ROD WITH ANIMAL FUR.

HOLD STILL!

PLACE THE CHARGED ROD IN A HANGING STIRRUP AND BRING ANOTHER, SIMILARLY CHARGED ROD NEAR — THEY **REPEL**.

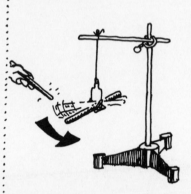

BUT IF I RUB A PLASTIC ROD WITH SILK...

IT ATTRACTS THE RUBBER ROD!

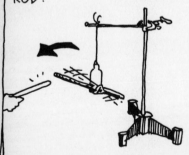

FROM EXPERIMENTS LIKE THESE WE LEARN THAT

THERE ARE **TWO** KINDS OF CHARGE...

AND THAT LIKE CHARGES REPEL, AND UNLIKE CHARGES ATTRACT!!

I LOVE SILK!

BENJAMIN FRANKLIN

(1706 · 1790) NAMED THE TWO KINDS OF CHARGES **POSITIVE** AND **NEGATIVE**. WE NOW KNOW THAT ALL MATTER IS MADE OF ATOMS, WHICH ARE COMPOSED OF NEGATIVELY CHARGED **ELECTRONS**, WHIRLING AROUND A NUCLEUS OF POSITIVELY CHARGED **PROTONS**, AND **NEUTRONS**, WHICH HAVE NO CHARGE.

ELECTRONS AND PROTONS HAVE EQUAL AND OPPOSITE CHARGES. NORMAL ATOMS HAVE EXACTLY ENOUGH ELECTRONS TO BALANCE THE PROTONS IN THE NUCLEUS, MAKING THE ATOM OVERALL NEUTRAL.

BUT WHEN AN ELECTRON IS REMOVED FROM AN ATOM, THE ATOM BECOMES A POSITIVELY CHARGED **ION**.

A CHARGED OBJECT WILL ALSO ATTRACT NEUTRAL OBJECTS. THIS RUBBER COMB, CHARGED NEGATIVELY BY RINGO'S HAIR, WILL PICK UP BITS OF PAPER.

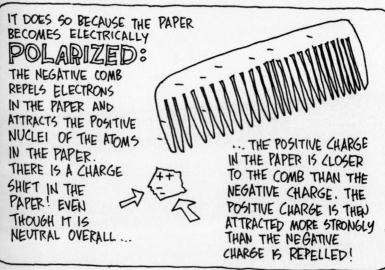

IT DOES SO BECAUSE THE PAPER BECOMES ELECTRICALLY **POLARIZED:** THE NEGATIVE COMB REPELS ELECTRONS IN THE PAPER AND ATTRACTS THE POSITIVE NUCLEI OF THE ATOMS IN THE PAPER. THERE IS A CHARGE SHIFT IN THE PAPER! EVEN THOUGH IT IS NEUTRAL OVERALL ...

... THE POSITIVE CHARGE IN THE PAPER IS CLOSER TO THE COMB THAN THE NEGATIVE CHARGE. THE POSITIVE CHARGE IS THEN ATTRACTED MORE STRONGLY THAN THE NEGATIVE CHARGE IS REPELLED!

FROM SUCH OBSERVATIONS, WE DEDUCE THAT THE ELECTRICAL FORCE **GROWS WEAKER WITH DISTANCE.**

NOT A WIGGLE!

WHEN YOU RUB THE RUBBER ROD WITH FUR, SOME ELECTRONS ARE RUBBED OFF THE FUR AND ONTO THE RUBBER, SO THE RUBBER ROD ACQUIRES A NET NEGATIVE CHARGE (LEAVING THE FUR POSITIVE).

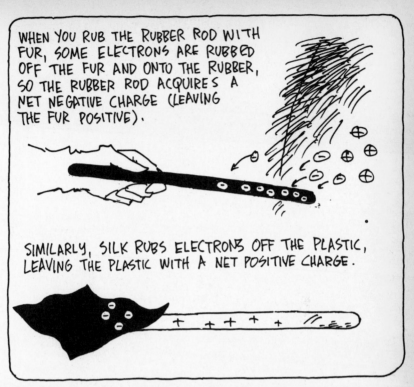

SIMILARLY, SILK RUBS ELECTRONS OFF THE PLASTIC, LEAVING THE PLASTIC WITH A NET POSITIVE CHARGE.

ELECTRONS ARE ELEMENTARY UNITS OF CHARGE, AND ARE EASILY TRANSFERRED FROM ONE OBJECT TO ANOTHER. THEY MAY ALSO BE PASSED ALONG THE SAME OBJECT — LIKE A COPPER WIRE, FOR EXAMPLE.

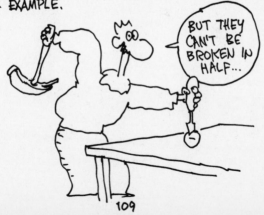

BUT THEY CAN'T BE BROKEN IN HALF...

MATERIALS LIKE RUBBER, GLASS, AND PLASTIC ARE ELECTRICAL

INSULATORS:

CHARGE CAN BE RUBBED ON OR OFF THEIR SURFACES, BUT IT TENDS TO STICK THERE AND WILL NOT MOVE EASILY THROUGH THE MATERIALS.

CORK

GLASS

RUBBER

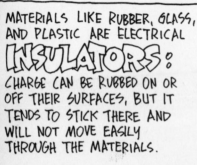

BUT IN METALS, LIKE COPPER, SILVER, AND ALUMINUM, THE ELECTRONS CAN MOVE AROUND FREELY AND EASILY. METALS ARE ELECTRICAL

CONDUCTORS.

WHAT WE CALL "ELECTRICITY" IS JUST A FLOW OF ELECTRONS.

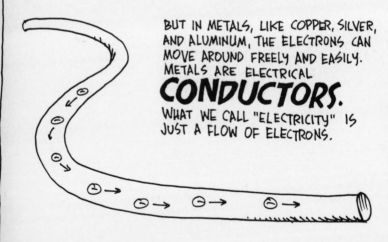

CAREFUL MEASUREMENTS BY CHARLES **COULOMB** (1736-1806) ESTABLISHED THAT THE ELECTRIC FORCE DECREASES WITH THE SQUARE OF THE DISTANCE, LIKE GRAVITY. COULOMB'S LAW FOR ELECTROSTATIC* FORCES IS VERY MUCH LIKE NEWTON'S LAW OF GRAVITY:

$$F = k \frac{Qq}{r^2}$$

*ELECTROSTATIC MEANS THAT THE CHARGES ARE STATIONARY.

IN COULOMB'S EQUATION, Q AND q ARE THE VALUES OF THE CHARGES, r IS THE DISTANCE BETWEEN THEM, AND k IS A CONSTANT, LIKE G FOR GRAVITY. IN STANDARD UNITS, $k = 9 \times 10^9$.

THE UNIT OF CHARGE IS THE **COULOMB.** A SINGLE ELECTRON HAS A CHARGE OF $-e = 1.6 \times 10^{-19}$ COULOMBS.

JUST HOW SIMILAR ARE THE GRAVITATIONAL AND ELECTROSTATIC FORCES?

ALTHOUGH THE LAW OF ELECTROSTATIC FORCES SEEMS VERY
SIMILAR TO THE LAW OF GRAVITY, THERE ARE MAJOR DIFFERENCES
BETWEEN THEM. FOR
EXAMPLE, GRAVITY
ALWAYS ATTRACTS,
BUT ELECTRICAL
FORCES CAN EITHER
ATTRACT OR REPEL.

ALSO, ELECTRICAL FORCES ARE VASTLY STRONGER THAN
GRAVITATIONAL FORCES. IF A (MERE!) HUNDRED BILLION
ELECTRONS WERE MOVED FROM A PLASTIC ROD TO A RUBBER
ONE, THERE IS A PERCEPTIBLE ATTRACTION BETWEEN THEM.

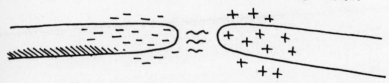

BUT EVEN WITH ALL 10^{24} (=10^{13} BILLION) ATOMS IN THE ROD
PULLING GRAVITATIONALLY, THE MOST SENSITIVE INSTRUMENTS
WOULD HAVE TROUBLE DETECTING IT!

CHEW ON THIS!

CHARGE IS CONSERVED — THE NET CHARGE, THE SUM OF THE NEGATIVE AND POSITIVE CHARGES IN AN ISOLATED SYSTEM CANNOT CHANGE.

(WHEN THE NEUTRAL RUBBER WAS CHARGED BY THE ANIMAL FUR, THE POSITIVE CHARGE ON THE FUR MATCHES THE NEGATIVE CHARGE ON THE RUBBER.)

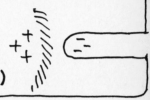

BUT!

IT IS POSSIBLE TO CREATE PAIRS OF CHARGES FROM **NOTHING**

NOTHING BUT ENERGY, THAT IS!

THIS IS DONE BY A **GAMMA RAY**, A VERY HIGH-ENERGY PARTICLE OF LIGHT. WHEN A GAMMA RAY PASSES NEAR AN ATOMIC NUCLEUS, IT MAY CREATE TWO PARTICLES — A NEGATIVE ELECTRON AND A POSITIVE POSITRON. THESE TWO MAY LATER ANNIHILATE EACH OTHER, PRODUCING MORE GAMMA RAYS.

GAMMA RAY

POSITRON

e+

e-

ELECTRON

NUCLEUS

e+

e-

GAMMA RAYS

BUT NO KNOWN PHYSICAL PROCESS CAN CREATE OR DESTROY A SINGLE CHARGE!

BUT WE'VE DISCOVERED SOME NOVEL HAIR-STRAIGHTENING TECHNIQUES...

DIE HARD

A PIECE OF ELECTROSTATIC APPARATUS YOU CAN MAKE FOR YOURSELF IS AN

ELECTROPHORUS.

INVENTED BY VOLTA IN 1775!

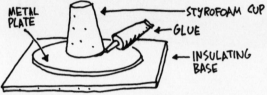

METAL PLATE

STYROFOAM CUP

GLUE

INSULATING BASE

YOU'LL NEED A PLASTIC PLATE FOR THE BASE AND A METAL PIE PLATE WITH AN INSULATING HANDLE, SAY A STYROFOAM CUP, GLUED TO IT.

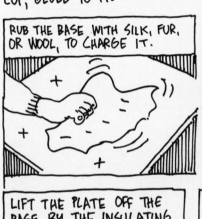

RUB THE BASE WITH SILK, FUR, OR WOOL, TO CHARGE IT.

NOW PLACE THE METAL PLATE ON THE BASE, AND TOUCH THE PLATE WITH YOUR FINGER.

LIFT THE PLATE OFF THE BASE BY THE INSULATING HANDLE.

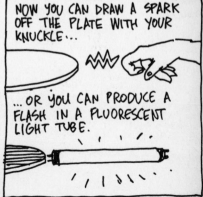

NOW YOU CAN DRAW A SPARK OFF THE PLATE WITH YOUR KNUCKLE...

...OR YOU CAN PRODUCE A FLASH IN A FLUORESCENT LIGHT TUBE.

AN INTERESTING FEATURE OF THIS EXPERIMENT IS THAT YOU CAN RECHARGE THE PLATE BY TOUCHING IT WITH YOUR FINGER REPEATEDLY, WITHOUT FURTHER RUBBING OF THE BASE.

HOW DOES THIS WORK? WHERE DOES THE ENERGY OF THE SPARK COME FROM IF THE CHARGE ON THE BASE IS NOT USED UP?

THE BASE IS CHARGED POSITIVE BY RUBBING. WHEN THE PLATE IS PLACED ON THE BASE, IT ACTUALLY TOUCHES IT IN ONLY A FEW PLACES:

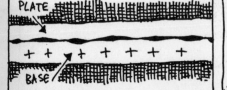

PLATE

+ + + + + + + +

BASE

SINCE THE BASE IS AN INSULATOR, VERY LITTLE CHARGE FLOWS. BUT WHEN YOU TOUCH THE METAL, ELECTRONS IN YOUR BODY, ATTRACTED BY THE POSITIVE BASE, FLOW ONTO THE PLATE, CHARGING IT NEGATIVE.

YOUR BODY SERVES AS AN **ELECTRICAL GROUND,** A RESERVOIR OF POSITIVE AND NEGATIVE CHARGES. SINCE THE CHARGE ON THE PLATE COMES FROM YOU, THE EXPERIMENT CAN BE REPEATED INDEFINITELY.

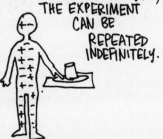

AND WHERE DOES THE SPARK'S ENERGY COME FROM? IT COMES FROM THE EXTRA FORCE YOU MUST EXERT TO LIFT THE NEGATIVE PLATE AWAY FROM THE POSITIVE BASE!

GRRUNT

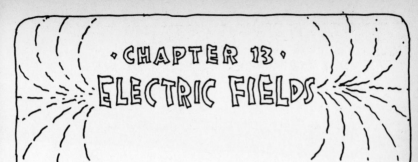

· CHAPTER 13 ·
ELECTRIC FIELDS

CONSIDER GRAVITATION!

THE EARTH EXERTS A FORCE ON THE MOON, A BODY THOUSANDS OF MILES AWAY. SIMILARLY, ONE ELECTRIC CHARGE EXERTS FORCES ON OTHER CHARGES WHICH ARE SEPARATED FROM IT IN SPACE.

HOW CAN ONE OBJECT EXERT A FORCE ON ANOTHER WHICH IT IS NOT TOUCHING? HOW CAN THE FORCE GET ACROSS SPACE? HOW FAST DOES IT GET THERE?

FASTER THAN A SPEEDING CAFFEINE ADDICT?

A BEGINNING OF THE ANSWER IS TO IMAGINE THAT THE EARTH FILLS SPACE WITH A **GRAVITATIONAL FIELD.** IT IS THE FIELD (WHATEVER IT IS!) THAT CAUSES THE FORCES ON MASSES WITHIN IT.

FIELD? WHUZZA FIELD?

DUN'T ESK!

SIMILARLY, A CHARGE FILLS SPACE WITH AN

ELECTRIC FIELD.

WHEN ANOTHER CHARGE IS IN THE ELECTRIC FIELD, ELECTRIC FORCES ACT ON IT!

FIELD? WHERE IZZIT?

IT FILLS SPACE!

WE CAN VISUALIZE THE ELECTRIC FIELD BY IMAGINING THAT WE ARE CARRYING A SMALL POSITIVE TEST CHARGE AROUND AND MAPPING THE DIRECTION OF THE FORCE ON IT. HERE, RINGO HAS A SINGLE POSITIVE CHARGE, AND I'M MOVING THE TEST CHARGE AROUND.

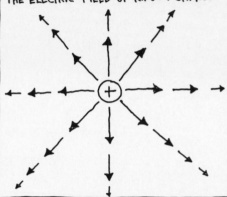

IF WE DRAW ARROWS IN THE DIRECTION OF THE FORCE, WITH LENGTH PROPORTIONAL TO ITS STRENGTH, WE GET A PICTURE OF THE ELECTRIC FIELD OF RINGO'S CHARGE:

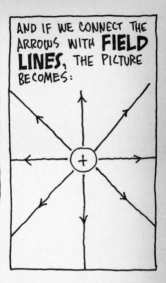

AND IF WE CONNECT THE ARROWS WITH **FIELD LINES**, THE PICTURE BECOMES:

FIELD LINES GIVE A VERY CONVINCING PICTURE OF ELECTRIC FIELDS; FOR EXAMPLE, FOR TWO ATTRACTING CHARGES:

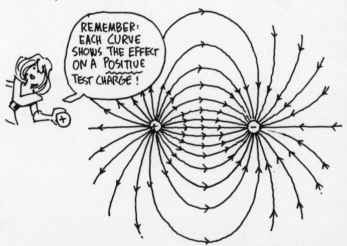

REMEMBER: EACH CURVE SHOWS THE EFFECT ON A POSITIVE TEST CHARGE!

THE FIELD LINES BEGIN AT THE POSITIVE CHARGE AND END AT THE NEGATIVE CHARGE: THE NEGATIVE CHARGE PULLS A POSITIVE TEST CHARGE IN FROM ANY DIRECTION.

SINCE THE ELECTRIC FIELD EXERTS FORCES ON CHARGES, THERE
IS ENERGY ASSOCIATED WITH THE POSITION OF A PARTICLE IN
THE FIELD. HERE RINGO HOLDS A POSITIVE CHARGE, AND,
STARTING FAR AWAY, I BRING A SMALL POSITIVE TEST
CHARGE IN CLOSE TO IT.

AS I MOVE IN, THE CHARGE IS REPELLED, SO I HAVE TO
EXERT FORCE TO PUSH IT CLOSER. FORCE TIMES DISTANCE
EQUALS **WORK** — I DO WORK ON THE TEST CHARGE.

WE SAY THAT THE WORK
GOES INTO THE

POTENTIAL
ENERGY

OF THE TEST CHARGE.
IF I RELEASE THE CHARGE, IT
FLIES AWAY, AND POTENTIAL ENERGY
IS CONVERTED INTO KINETIC ENERGY.

ZIP

WE WOULD LIKE TO ATTRIBUTE THE POTENTIAL ENERGY SOLELY TO THE ELECTRIC FIELD OF RINGO'S CHARGE, SO WE DIVIDE OUT MY TEST CHARGE AND WRITE:

$$\text{Potential} = \frac{\text{POTENTIAL ENERGY}}{\text{CHARGE}}$$

A FORMULA FOR MY POTENTIAL... AH!

THIS EQUATION DEFINES A NEW QUANTITY, THE ELECTRIC POTENTIAL.* POTENTIAL MEASURES ENERGY PER CHARGE. ITS UNITS ARE JOULES PER COULOMB, WHICH WE GIVE A NAME ALL ITS OWN, THE **VOLT**.

$$1 \text{ Volt} = 1 \frac{\text{JOULE}}{\text{COULOMB}}$$

AS WITH ANY NEW DEFINITION IN PHYSICS, IT IS IMPORTANT TO UNDERSTAND THE BASIC CONCEPT.

IF A BATTERY IS RATED AT 6 VOLTS, THAT MEANS IT IS PREPARED TO GIVE 6 JOULES OF ENERGY TO EVERY COULOMB THAT IS MOVED FROM ONE TERMINAL TO THE OTHER.

* THERE IS ALSO A GRAVITATIONAL POTENTIAL. IF P.E. $= mgh$, THEN $\frac{\text{P.E.}}{m} = gh$ IS THE ABILITY OF THE GRAVITATIONAL FIELD TO TRANSMIT ENERGY TO ANY MASS AT HEIGHT h.

O.K... SO HERE'S A CHARGE... BUT I STILL DON'T GET IT...

WHAT **IS** A CHARGE, ANYWAY?? I MEAN, IT MUST BE SOMETHING — MUSN'T IT...?

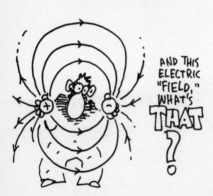
AND THIS ELECTRIC "FIELD," WHAT'S **THAT**?

HOW CAN IT "CARRY" A FORCE? HOW CAN SOME **IDEA** THAT "FILLS SPACE" CARRY **ANYTHING** ??

I'M JUST AS CONFUSED AS EVER!!

HMM..

SORRY, RINGO, OLD BOY, BUT YOU HAVE A POINT... CLASSICAL E & M NEVER ANSWERS THOSE QUESTIONS. IT ONLY DESCRIBES HOW CHARGES AND FIELDS BEHAVE... BUT IF YOU CAN HANG ON UNTIL THE END OF THE BOOK, I'LL TELL YOU A LITTLE ABOUT WHAT QUANTUM THEORY SAYS CHARGES AND FIELDS "REALLY ARE..."

·CHAPTER 14·
+CAPACITORS+

A CAPACITOR CONSISTS OF
TWO CONDUCTORS SEPARATED
BY AN INSULATOR, FOR
EXAMPLE, TWO METAL PLATES
WITH AIR BETWEEN THEM.

ELECTRIC
SYMBOL

A CAPACITOR IS CHARGED BY REMOVING SOME CHARGE
FROM ONE PLATE AND PLACING IT ON THE OTHER.

THE EASIEST
WAY TO DO THIS
IS TO CONNECT
THE CAPACITOR
BRIEFLY TO A
BATTERY. THE
BATTERY PUMPS
CHARGE FROM
ONE PLATE TO
THE OTHER.

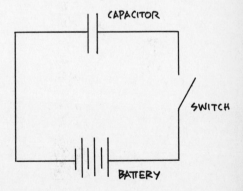

CAPACITOR

SWITCH

BATTERY

123

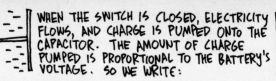

WHEN THE SWITCH IS CLOSED, ELECTRICITY FLOWS, AND CHARGE IS PUMPED ONTO THE CAPACITOR. THE AMOUNT OF CHARGE PUMPED IS PROPORTIONAL TO THE BATTERY'S VOLTAGE. SO WE WRITE:

$$Q = CV$$

CHARGE = CONSTANT · VOLTAGE

THE CONSTANT OF PROPORTIONALITY C IS A NUMBER DEPENDING ON THE CHARACTERISTICS OF THE CAPACITOR. IT IS CALLED THE **CAPACITANCE.**

CAPACITANCE IS MEASURED IN **FARADS,** AFTER MICHAEL **FARADAY** (1791·1867). THE HIGHER THE CAPACITANCE, THE MORE CHARGE THE CAPACITOR CAN STORE.

CAPACITANCE, IN TURN, IS DIRECTLY PROPORTIONAL TO THE AREA OF THE PLATES, AND INVERSELY PROPORTIONAL TO THE SEPARATION BETWEEN THEM. THE BIGGER AND CLOSER THE PLATES, THE MORE CHARGE THEY WILL HOLD.

THEY ATTRACT EACH OTHER, SEE?

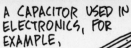

A CAPACITOR USED IN ELECTRONICS, FOR EXAMPLE,

MIGHT BE TWO ALUMINUM SHEETS SEPARATED A TINY DISTANCE BY SPECIAL CHEMICALS...

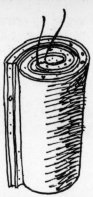

...AND ROLLED UP INTO A COMPACT TUBULAR PACKAGE.

AFTER THE CAPACITOR IS CHARGED, IT CAN BE DISCONNECTED FROM THE BATTERY, AND IT WILL REMAIN CHARGED FOR MINUTES, OR EVEN HOURS, ALTHOUGH CHARGE WILL SLOWLY LEAK INTO THE AIR.

BUT, IF I NOW CAREFULLY BRING THE LEADS OF THE CAPACITOR TOGETHER... THE CHARGE FLOWS AROUND THE WIRES AND NEUTRALIZES THE PLATES. THIS IS CALLED DISCHARGING THE CAPACITOR."

BANG!

THIS SHOWS HOW CAPACITORS CAN BE USED TO STORE
CHARGE AND ENERGY.
FOR EXAMPLE, A
PHOTOGRAPHER'S
ELECTRONIC FLASH
UNIT HAS A LARGE
CAPACITOR TO STORE
ENERGY FOR THE
FLASH TUBE. THE
BATTERY TAKES
ABOUT 30 SECONDS
TO CHARGE IT UP.

THEN, WHEN THE CHARGE IS NEEDED, ALL OF IT IS
DUMPED THROUGH THE FLASH TUBE IN AN INSTANT!

SAY "CAPACITOR!"

WHEN THE CAPACITOR IS CHARGED, POSITIVE AND NEGATIVE
CHARGES FACE EACH OTHER AND HOLD EACH OTHER IN
PLACE ACROSS THE INSULATOR —AND OF COURSE THERE
IS AN ELECTRIC FIELD!

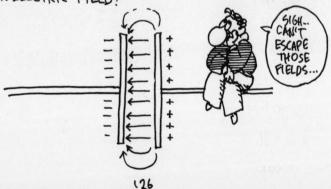

SIGH...
CAN'T
ESCAPE
THOSE
FIELDS...

IF AN ELECTRON IS RELEASED NEAR THE NEGATIVE PLATE, THE ELECTRIC FIELD WILL ACCELERATE IT TOWARD THE POSITIVE PLATE. IN FACT, IF WE MAKE A SMALL HOLE IN THE POSITIVE PLATE, THE ELECTRON WILL ZIP THROUGH:

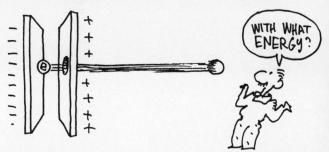

WITH WHAT ENERGY?

HERE WE MAKE UP A NEW ENERGY UNIT: THE

ELECTRON VOLT (eV).

WHEN IN DOUBT, INVENT A UNIT!

IT'S THE ENERGY OF ONE ELECTRON IF THE PLATES ARE CHARGED TO ONE VOLT. IF THE PLATES HAVE 100 VOLTS, THE ELECTRON WILL HAVE 100 eV...

ETC.!

TO CONVERT eV TO JOULES, WE USE THE DEFINITION POTENTIAL = ENERGY / CHARGE:

. . . .

1 eV = CHARGE OF ELECTRON
$\times$
1 VOLT

$= 1.6 \times 10^{-19} C \times 1 \ J/C$

$= 1.6 \times 10^{-19}$ JOULES

(THAT'S .00000000000000000016 !)

USING MODERN HI-TECH, WE CAN NOW ACCELERATE CHARGES TO MILLIONS OF ELECTRON VOLTS. BUT AT THESE ENERGIES, ELECTRONS ARE GOING CLOSE TO THE SPEED OF LIGHT, AND RELATIVITY THEORY MUST BE USED TO DESCRIBE THEM.

ME AGAIN!

· CHAPTER 15 ·
ELECTRIC CURRENTS

THE GREATEST ACHIEVEMENT OF THE ITALIAN PHYSICIST ALESSANDRO GIUSEPPE ANTONIO ANASTASIO **VOLTA**, ASIDE FROM REMEMBERING HIS OWN NAME, WAS THE INVENTION OF THE ELECTRIC BATTERY IN 1794.

GIUSEPPE ANTONIO?

ANTONIO GIUSEPPE?

VOLTA FOUND THAT IF YOU DIP TWO DIFFERENT METALS IN A CHEMICAL BATH, A DIFFERENCE IN POTENTIAL WILL APPEAR BETWEEN THEM.

CALL IT A **VOLTAGE!**

GRAZIE!

POTENTIAL HERE

ACID

THIS MEANS THAT CHARGE "WANTS TO" MOVE FROM ONE METAL TERMINAL TO THE OTHER. IF YOU CONNECTED THEM WITH A WIRE, CHARGE WOULD FLOW THROUGH IT.

HERE'S A SIMPLE "VOLTAIC CELL" WITH ALMOST ONE FULL VOLT OF POTENTIAL: A LEMON WITH TWO NAILS!

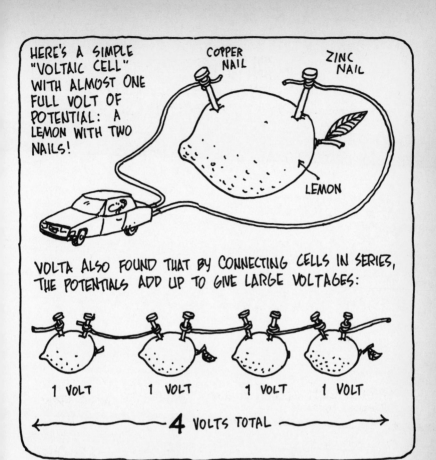

COPPER NAIL

ZINC NAIL

LEMON

VOLTA ALSO FOUND THAT BY CONNECTING CELLS IN SERIES, THE POTENTIALS ADD UP TO GIVE LARGE VOLTAGES:

1 VOLT   1 VOLT   1 VOLT   1 VOLT

← **4** VOLTS TOTAL →

A FLASHLIGHT "BATTERY" IS ACTUALLY A SINGLE CHEMICAL CELL. A TRUE BATTERY, LIKE THE ONE IN YOUR CAR, CONSISTS OF SEVERAL CELLS CONNECTED IN SERIES, AS ABOVE. THEIR ELECTRICAL SYMBOLS ARE:

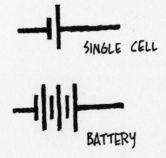

SINGLE CELL

BATTERY

LET'S HOOK UP A SIMPLE CIRCUIT: A BATTERY WIRED TO A LIGHT BULB.

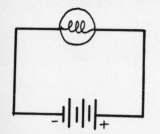

THE BATTERY CONTINUALLY "PUMPS" CHARGE AROUND THE CIRCUIT, LIGHTING THE BULB.

WE CALL THIS FLOW OF CHARGE THE

CURRENT.

I FEEL A NEW UNIT COMING ON...

CURRENT IS MEASURED IN COULOMBS PER SECOND, ALSO KNOWN AS:

amperes.

WE OFTEN DRAW AN ARROW ALONG THE WIRE, LEADING FROM THE BATTERY'S POSITIVE TERMINAL TO THE NEGATIVE, AS IF POSITIVE CHARGES FLOWED THAT WAY. THIS IS CALLED "CONVENTIONAL CURRENT," AS OPPOSED TO REAL CURRENT, WHICH IS A FLOW OF NEGATIVE ELECTRONS IN THE OPPOSITE DIRECTION. IN MOST ELECTRICAL EFFECTS, THERE IS NO WAY TO DISTINGUISH BETWEEN THESE TWO POSSIBILITIES.

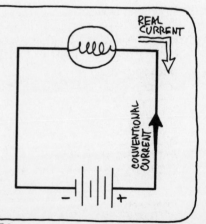

REAL CURRENT

CONVENTIONAL CURRENT

TO KEEP ALL THESE CONCEPTS IN MIND, IT HELPS TO HAVE A MECHANICAL ANALOGY:

YES, PLEASE.

IMAGINE THAT ELECTRIC CURRENT IS LIKE WATER FLOWING THROUGH A PIPE. THEN WE HAVE THESE CORRESPONDENCES:

ELECTRICITY	WATER
COULOMB OF CHARGE	LITER OF WATER
AMPERE	ONE LITER/SEC FLOW
BATTERY	PUMP
VOLTAGE	PUMP PRESSURE
WIRE	PIPE

THE LAMP FILAMENT IS LIKE A SECTION OF PIPE FILLED WITH GRAVEL THAT **RESISTS** THE FLOW OF WATER. IN FACT, THE FRICTION OF FLOWING WATER EVEN HEATS THE GRAVEL!

TO GET A LARGE FLOW, OR CURRENT, A HIGH PRESSURE, OR VOLTAGE, IS REQUIRED. GEORGE OHM (1789-1854) SUMMARIZED THIS RELATION AS OHM'S LAW:

$$i = \frac{V}{R}$$

CURRENT, i, EQUALS VOLTAGE, V, DIVIDED BY RESISTANCE R. THE HIGHER THE VOLTAGE, THE MORE CURRENT FLOWS THROUGH A GIVEN RESISTANCE.

(OHM'S LAW IS NOT UNIVERSALLY TRUE, LIKE COULOMB'S LAW, BUT IS APPROXIMATELY TRUE IN MANY SITUATIONS.)

RESISTANCE IS MEASURED IN **OHMS.**
IT DEPENDS ON THE MATERIAL, THE
AREA THROUGH WHICH CURRENT
FLOWS, AND THE LENGTH
IT MUST TRAVEL.

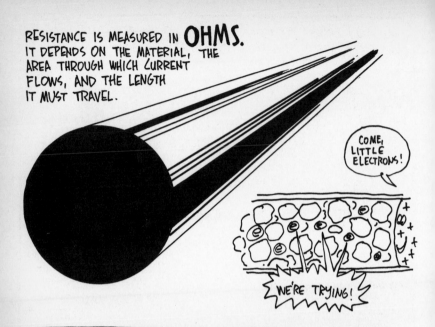

COME, LITTLE ELECTRONS!

WE'RE TRYING!

THINK AGAIN OF WATER FLOWING THROUGH A PIPEFUL OF GRAVEL.
A SECTION OF PIPE TWICE AS LONG HAS TWICE THE RESISTANCE...
A WIDER PIPE HAS LESS RESISTANCE, BECAUSE IT OFFERS MORE
SPACES FOR WATER TO FLOW... AND RESISTANCE DEPENDS ON
THE TYPE OF GRAVEL.

LONG PIPE,
HIGH RESISTANCE

SHORT PIPE,
LOW RESISTANCE

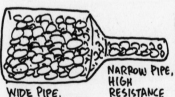

WIDE PIPE,
LOW RESISTANCE

NARROW PIPE,
HIGH
RESISTANCE

SMOOTH GRAVEL, LOW RESISTANCE

ROUGH GRAVEL, HIGH RESISTANCE

LIKEWISE, AN ELECTRIC WIRE'S RESISTANCE IS PROPORTIONAL TO ITS
LENGTH AND INVERSELY PROPORTIONAL TO ITS CROSS-SECTIONAL AREA.

AND, LIKE DIFFERENT TYPES OF GRAVEL, DIFFERENT MATERIALS HAVE DIFFERENT INTRINSIC **RESISTIVITY**. GOOD CONDUCTORS HAVE LOW RESISTIVITY:

HUP!

GOOD CONDUCTORS WITH LOW RESISTIVITY: SILVER, GOLD, COPPER, ALUMINUM

DON'T WANNA...

POOR CONDUCTORS WITH HIGH RESISTIVITY: PLASTIC, PAPER, CLOTH

A LAMP FILAMENT IS LIKELY TO BE MADE OF **TUNGSTEN,** WHICH HAS A MUCH HIGHER RESISTIVITY THAN COPPER — HENCE A GREATER RESISTANCE THAN THE SAME SIZE COPPER WIRE.

(YOU WANT HIGH RESISTANCE IN A LIGHT BULB, SO THAT IT "DISSIPATES" ELECTRIC ENERGY AS LIGHT!)

YES, THE BULB DOES GO OFF WHEN YOU CLOSE THE DOOR...

RESISTIVITY ALSO CHANGES WITH TEMPERATURE. FOR MOST MATERIALS, IT RISES SLOWLY WITH TEMPERATURE, AS VIBRATING MOLECULES INTERFERE WITH THE FLOW OF CHARGE.

133

FOR SOME MATERIALS, LIKE MERCURY AND ALUMINUM, THE RESISTIVITY FALLS TO

ZERO

AT VERY COLD TEMPERATURES. NEAR ABSOLUTE ZERO (−273° CENTIGRADE), THESE MATERIALS CONDUCT ELECTRICITY WITHOUT ANY RESISTANCE AT ALL. THEN THEY ARE CALLED

superconductors.

NO RESISTANCE? THEY CATCH COLD EASILY?

THEY'RE ALREADY COLD...

THE WONDERFUL THING ABOUT SUPERCONDUCTORS IS THAT THEY CAN CARRY HUGE CURRENTS WITHOUT ANY LOSS TO HEAT. THESE CURRENTS CAN EVEN PERSIST FOR YEARS WITHOUT LOSS OF ENERGY. SUPERCONDUCTORS, THOUGH EXPENSIVE, ARE USED IN PARTICLE ACCELERATORS, WHERE SUPER-STRONG ELECTROMAGNETS REQUIRE GIANT ELECTRIC CURRENTS.

AND EVEN BIGGER BUDGETS!

IN 1986, SCIENTISTS DISCOVERED SEVERAL NEW SUPERCONDUCTING COMPOUNDS THAT LOSE THEIR RESISTIVITY AT MUCH HIGHER TEMPERATURES, AROUND −180° C. THIS MAY SOUND COLD, BUT IT'S A WARM BATH COMPARED WITH ABSOLUTE ZERO.

THESE COMPOUNDS CAN BE CHILLED WITH INEXPENSIVE LIQUID NITROGEN... SO WE MAY SEE SOME AMAZING COMMERCIAL APPLICATIONS IN THE COMING YEARS, SUCH AS LEVITATING TRAINS...

NOW BACK TO OUR SIMPLE
CIRCUIT, A SMALL LIGHT BULB
CONNECTED BY COPPER WIRE
TO A 6-VOLT BATTERY.

THE LAMP FILAMENT MIGHT HAVE 6 OHMS OF RESISTANCE,
IN WHICH CASE, BY OHM'S LAW, THE CURRENT WOULD BE

$$i = \frac{V}{R} = \frac{6 \text{ VOLTS}}{6 \text{ OHMS}} = 1 \text{ AMPERE}$$

YOU FORGOT
THE RESISTANCE
OF THE
WIRE...

(COPPER WIRE'S
RESISTANCE IS NEGLIGIBLE—
LESS THAN $\frac{1}{100}$ OHM —
CONTRIBUTING LITTLE
TO THE OVERALL
RESISTANCE *)

THE QUESTION IS, HOW WOULD
YOU MEASURE THESE QUANTITIES
IN THE CIRCUIT?

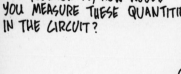

1. REMOVE BULB.
2. INSERT FINGER
   IN SOCKET.
3. MEASURE
   RESULTANT
   HAIR CURL...?

*UNLESS THE WIRE IS VERY LONG OR VERY THIN.

FOR AS LITTLE AS TEN DOLLARS, YOU CAN BUY A **MULTIMETER** THAT WILL MEASURE VOLTAGE, CURRENT, AND RESISTANCE.

AND FOR $7995.29, YOU CAN GET 4 WHEEL DRIVE AND AM-FM CASETTE!

TO MEASURE VOLTAGE, TOUCH THE METER'S LEADS **ACROSS** THE LAMP OR BATTERY. TOUCHING IT ACROSS THE LAMP MEASURES THE **VOLTAGE DROP** OF THE LAMP.

VOLTAGE WHAT?

THE VOLTAGE "DROP" REFERS TO THE ENERGY PER CHARGE THAT IS GOING INTO HEAT AND LIGHT.

DO YOU NEED A LICENSE FOR THIS?

IF YOU TOUCHED THE LEADS TO THE WIRE ON THE SAME SIDE OF THE LAMP, YOU'D GET A NEAR-ZERO READING. IT TAKES ALMOST NO VOLTAGE TO PUSH CURRENT THROUGH A COPPER WIRE. AND MEASURING ACROSS THE BATTERY GIVES ITS VOLTAGE "STEP-UP," THE ENERGY PER UNIT CHARGE PUMPED INTO THE CIRCUIT BY THE BATTERY.

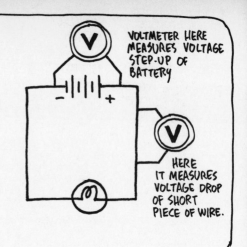

VOLTMETER HERE MEASURES VOLTAGE STEP-UP OF BATTERY

HERE IT MEASURES VOLTAGE DROP OF SHORT PIECE OF WIRE.

TO MEASURE **CURRENT**, YOU MUST BREAK THE CIRCUIT AND INSERT THE AMMETER.

THE SAME CURRENT IS FLOWING EVERYWHERE IN THIS SIMPLE CIRCUIT, AND WE MUST MAKE IT FLOW THROUGH THE AMMETER TO BE MEASURED.

NEXT TIME I MUST REMEMBER MY RUBBER SEAT COVERS...

138

AND RESISTANCE?

YOU COULD MEASURE THE LAMP FILAMENT'S RESISTANCE DIRECTLY, BY TAKING IT OUT OF THE CIRCUIT AND TESTING IT WITH THE OHMMETER SETTING OF THE MULTIMETER.

$$R = \frac{V}{i}$$

OR YOU COULD USE THE PREVIOUS VOLTAGE AND CURRENT READINGS TO CALCULATE THE RESISTANCE WITH OHM'S LAW.

THESE TWO MEASUREMENTS WOULD ACTUALLY GIVE SOMEWHAT DIFFERENT RESULTS, SINCE WHEN THE BULB IS IN CIRCUIT, THE FILAMENT IS AT HIGH TEMPERATURE (AND HIGHER RESISTANCE), WHEREAS WHEN IT IS MEASURED WITH THE METER, THE FILAMENT IS COOL.

6 VOLTS / 0.9 AMPS = 6.6 OHMS

ANOTHER FAMILIAR ELECTRICAL UNIT IS THE

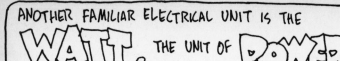

WATT, THE UNIT OF POWER.

POWER IS WHAT?

EXACTLY.

POWER IS DEFINED AS **ENERGY** PER UNIT OF TIME. IT MEASURES HOW FAST ENERGY IS PRODUCED OR CONSUMED. POWER APPLIES ALSO TO MECHANICAL SYSTEMS, AS IN A POWERFUL CAR, WHICH CAN ACCELERATE RAPIDLY. A HIGH-POWERED LIGHT BULB PUTS OUT A LOT OF LIGHT PER SECOND.

 BY DEFINITION, A **WATT** IS ONE **JOULE PER SECOND** — SO WE CAN RELATE WATTS TO VOLTS AND AMPS.

$$POWER = WATTS = \frac{JOULES}{SEC} =$$

$$\frac{JOULES}{COULOMB} \times \frac{COULOMBS}{SECOND} =$$

VOLTS × AMPS

THE PRODUCT OF **VOLTAGE** TIMES **CURRENT** IS **POWER**:

$$P = Vi$$

WATTS = VOLTS x AMPS

AND NO HORSIN' AROUND!

IN THE CASE OF OUR 6-OHM BULB ATTACHED TO A 6-VOLT BATTERY, WE HAVE ONE AMP OF CURRENT, AND THE POWER IS

$$P = 6 \text{ VOLTS} \times 1 \text{ AMP}$$

$$= 6 \text{ WATTS.}$$

DIM, BUT WE'LL SEE MORE LATER...

CHAPTER 16:
SERIES AND PARALLEL

I NOW PUT THREE
EQUAL LIGHT BULBS IN
SERIES WITH
A BATTERY. THIS
MEANS THEY ARE
WIRED TOGETHER
ONE AFTER THE
OTHER.

BY OUR MECHANICAL ANALOGY,
EACH LAMP FILAMENT IS LIKE
A GRAVEL·FILLED SECTION OF PIPE.
NOW THE CURRENT HAS THREE TIMES
AS MUCH GRAVEL TO FLOW THROUGH—

THREE
TIMES THE
RESISTANCE!*

*WE ARE ASSUMING THAT A LAMP'S RESISTANCE IS INDEPENDENT
OF CURRENT THROUGH THE LAMP, WHICH IS REALLY NOT THE CASE,
SINCE TEMPERATURE OF THE FILAMENT DEPENDS STRONGLY ON CURRENT.

OHM...

$$i = \frac{V}{R}$$

TRIPLING THE RESISTANCE MEANS THAT ONLY ONE THIRD THE CURRENT CAN FLOW. THE CURRENT MUST BE THE SAME IN EACH LIGHT, OF COURSE: THERE IS NOWHERE ELSE FOR THE CHARGE TO GO, AND IT DOESN'T ACCUMULATE IN THE CIRCUIT.

WHEN I TOUCH THE LEADS OF A VOLTMETER ACROSS ONE THE LAMPS, THE <u>VOLTAGE</u> <u>DROP</u> ACROSS THE LAMP IS ONE THIRD OF THE BATTERY VOLTAGE.

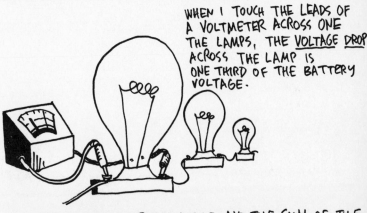

THE LAMPS DIVIDE UP THE VOLTAGE, AND THE SUM OF THE VOLTAGE DROPS ACROSS THE SERIES COMPONENTS MUST EQUAL THE BATTERY VOLTAGE.

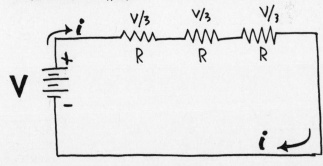

IN THE MORE GENERAL CASE, WITH UNEQUAL RESISTANCES IN SERIES, THE VOLTAGE DROPS V_1, V_2, AND V_3 REPRESENT ENERGY CONSUMED BY THE LAMPS,* ENERGY CONVERTED FROM ELECTRIC ENERGY INTO LIGHT AND HEAT.

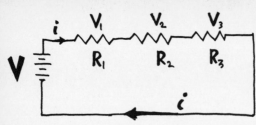

THE TOTAL ENERGY CONSUMED BY THE LAMPS MUST EQUAL THE ENERGY PRODUCED BY THE BATTERY, SO THESE VOLTAGE DROPS MUST ADD TO THE BATTERY VOLTAGE. THIS IS CALLED THE LOOP THEOREM, OR KIRKHHOFF'S FIRST LAW:

$$V = V_1 + V_2 + V_3$$

(AND $V_1 = iR_1$, ETC.)

IN SERIES, EACH OF THE THREE EQUAL LAMPS GETS ONE THIRD OF THE ORIGINAL CURRENT AT ONE THIRD THE VOLTAGE. SINCE POWER IS VOLTAGE TIMES CURRENT, EACH BULB IS ONE NINTH AS BRIGHT AS ONE BULB CONNECTED ALONE!

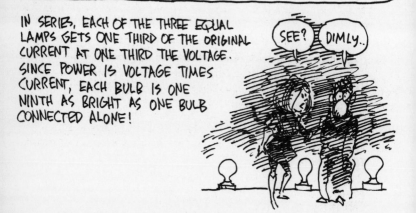

* REMEMBER, VOLTAGE IS ENERGY PER CHARGE.

NOW LET'S CONNECT THE BULBS IN **PARALLEL**:

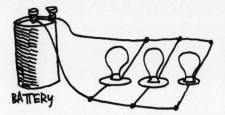

EACH LAMP IS CONNECTED DIRECTLY TO THE BATTERY, WITH NO OTHER BULB INTERVENING.

BATTERY

THIS WAY EVERY BULB GETS A FULL DOSE OF VOLTAGE, AND SHINES WITH ITS NORMAL BRIGHTNESS. THIS IS THE WAY A HOUSE WOULD NORMALLY BE WIRED SO THAT EVERY ELECTRIC FIXTURE GETS FULL HOUSE VOLTAGE.

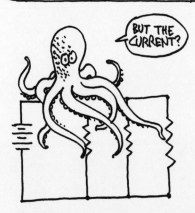

BUT THE CURRENT?

IN THE PARALLEL CIRCUIT, THE **CURRENT** HAS TO DIVIDE AND FLOW THROUGH THE THREE BRANCHES.

WHERE DID THAT OCTOPUS COME FROM?

A PARALLEL UNIVERSE?

BUT THE TOTAL **RESISTANCE** OF THE CIRCUIT IS ONE THIRD THAT OF ONE BULB — THERE IS THREE TIMES AS MUCH "AREA OF GRAVEL" TO FLOW THROUGH. THIS MAKES IT EASIER!

THEN, BY OHM'S LAW, THREE TIMES AS MUCH CURRENT CAN FLOW THROUGH THE CIRCUIT AS A WHOLE.

TO SUM UP, IN PARALLEL EACH COMPONENT GETS THE SAME VOLTAGE, AND DRAWS A CURRENT i INVERSELY PROPORTIONAL TO ITS RESISTANCE, BY OHM'S LAW $i = \dfrac{V}{R}$.

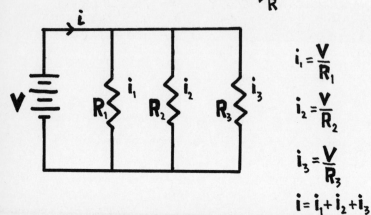

$$i_1 = \frac{V}{R_1}$$

$$i_2 = \frac{V}{R_2}$$

$$i_3 = \frac{V}{R_3}$$

$$i = i_1 + i_2 + i_3$$

WHAT IS THE CURRENT IN DIFFERENT PARTS OF THE CIRCUIT? THE CURRENT FLOWING INTO ANY JUNCTION IN THE CIRCUIT MUST EQUAL THE SUM OF THE CURRENTS FLOWING OUT. CURRENT IS THE FLOW OF CHARGE, WHICH IS CONSERVED.

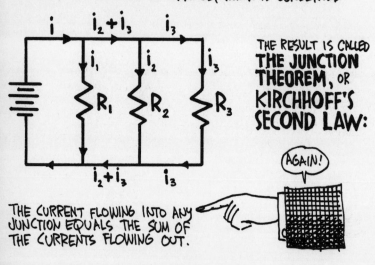

THE RESULT IS CALLED **THE JUNCTION THEOREM**, OR **KIRCHHOFF'S SECOND LAW:**

AGAIN!

THE CURRENT FLOWING INTO ANY JUNCTION EQUALS THE SUM OF THE CURRENTS FLOWING OUT.

HERE IS AN INTERESTING

PARADOX:

I'M GOING TO HOOK UP A 60-WATT BULB AND A 100-WATT BULB IN SERIES.

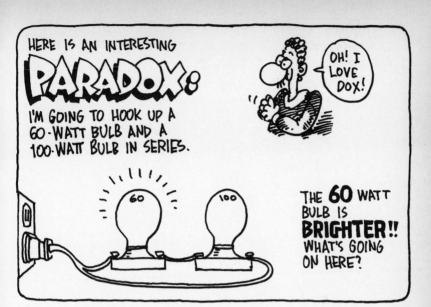

OH! I LOVE DOX!

THE **60** WATT BULB IS **BRIGHTER!!** WHAT'S GOING ON HERE?

FIRST, REMEMBER THAT THE WATT RATINGS ARE GOOD ONLY IF THE BULBS ARE PLUGGED IN ALONE, NOT IN SERIES.

IN SERIES, THEY DIVIDE UP THE VOLTAGE!

HOW MUCH VOLTAGE DOES EACH BULB IN SERIES GET? BOTH BULBS GET THE SAME CURRENT i, SO OHM'S LAW

$V = iR$ GIVES

THE VOLTAGE DROP ACROSS EACH BULB.

SO? WHERE ARE THE DOX?

NOW THE 60-WATT BULB HAS GREATER RESISTANCE: WHEN PLUGGED IN ALONE, IT DRAWS LESS CURRENT AND GLOWS LESS BRIGHTLY.

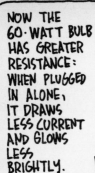

THE 100-WATT BULB, WITH LESS RESISTANCE, DRAWS MORE CURRENT WHEN PLUGGED IN ALONE.

VERY LOGICAL!

BUT IN **SERIES,** THE 60-WATT BULB, WITH HIGHER RESISTANCE, GETS **MORE VOLTAGE...**

...WHILE THE 100-WATT BULB GETS LESS!

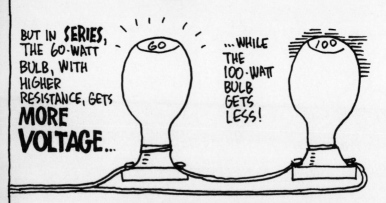

SO THE ACTUAL POWER **P = Vi** DELIVERED TO EACH LAMP IS HIGHER FOR THE 60-WATT BULB THAN FOR THE 100!

GET IT, RINGO?

YES... YOU DON'T HAVE TO TELL ME... THERE NEVER **WERE** ANY DOX...

·CHAPTER 17·

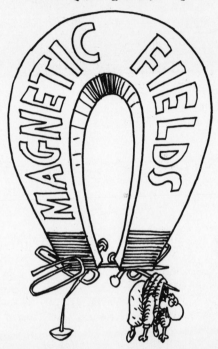

MAGNETIC FIELDS

SEVERAL THOUSAND YEARS AGO, THE GREEKS DISCOVERED THAT CERTAIN METALLIC ROCKS FROM THE DISTRICT OF **MAGNESIA** IN ASIA MINOR WOULD ATTRACT IRON, AND ATTRACT OR REPEL SIMILAR ROCKS. HENCE THE NAME "MAGNET..."

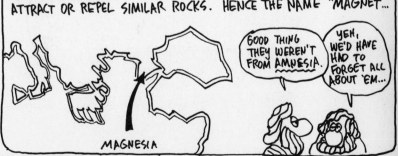

GOOD THING THEY WEREN'T FROM AMNESIA.

YEH, WE'D HAVE HAD TO FORGET ALL ABOUT 'EM...

MAGNESIA

FURTHER STUDY ESTABLISHED THAT MAGNETS ALWAYS HAVE TWO **POLES,** CALLED **NORTH** AND **SOUTH.**

N S

IF YOU ALLOW A MAGNET TO PIVOT, ITS **NORTH** POLE IS THE ONE THAT POINTS TOWARD THE EARTH'S (GEOGRAPHIC) NORTH.

A **COMPASS** IS JUST A MAGNETIC NEEDLE ON A PIVOT.

WE ALSO NOTE THAT UNLIKE POLES ATTRACT, WHILE LIKE POLES REPEL.

NOW IMAGINE THAT WE HAD SCATTERED TINY COMPASS NEEDLES ON A SHEET OF PAPER AND BROUGHT A BAR MAGNET UNDERNEATH THEM:

THE NEEDLES WILL LINE UP, REVEALING THE BAR MAGNET'S

MAGNETIC FIELD.

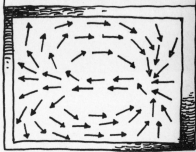

AS WITH THE ELECTRIC FIELD, WE CONNECT THE LINES ALONG THE DIRECTION OF THE ARROWS AND SEE THE RESULTING MAGNETIC **FIELD LINES.**

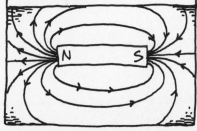

BY CONVENTION, WE AGREE THAT THE FIELD LINES EMERGE FROM THE **NORTH** MAGNETIC POLE AND POINT TOWARD THE **SOUTH** MAGNETIC POLE.

(NOTE THAT THIS MAKES THE EARTH'S SOUTH MAGNETIC POLE BE THE ONE IN THE GEOGRAPHIC NORTH!)

YOU WOULD FIND THAT BREAKING THE MAGNET GENERATES TWO NEW POLES! YOU CAN NEVER ISOLATE A POLE FROM ITS OPPOSITE.

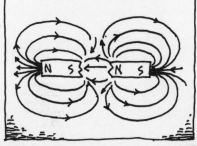

ALSO, THE FIELD LINES DON'T STOP OR END, BUT PASS THROUGH THE MAGNET FROM SOUTH TO NORTH, FORMING CLOSED CURVES.

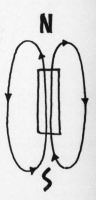

UP UNTIL THE YEAR
1820
EVERYONE THOUGHT MAGNETISM AND ELECTRICITY WERE COMPLETELY SEPARATE.

ELECTRICITY? MAGNETISM? TO DO? WITH EACH OTHER? SOMETHING? HA HA HA HA

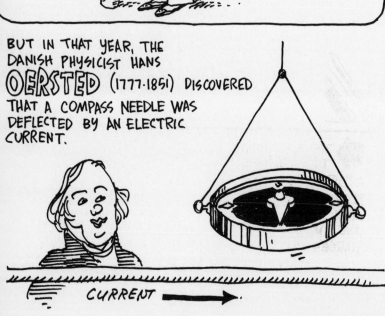

BUT IN THAT YEAR, THE DANISH PHYSICIST HANS **OERSTED** (1777-1851) DISCOVERED THAT A COMPASS NEEDLE WAS DEFLECTED BY AN ELECTRIC CURRENT.

CURRENT ➡

152

Q: WHAT DOES A CHARGE FEEL IN A MAGNETIC FIELD?

RAGE?

JEALOUSY?

PITY?

FIRST, IF THE CHARGE IS NOT MOVING, THERE IS **NO FORCE.**

NOT A THING!

...AND THERE IS NO FORCE IF THE CHARGE IS MOVING **ALONG** A FIELD LINE...

STILL NOTHIN'!

...BUT IF THE CHARGE IS MOVING **ACROSS** THE FIELD LINES, IT FEELS SOMETHING!

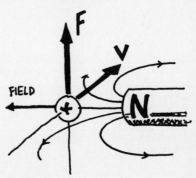

YI!

➤ THE FORCE ON THE CHARGE IS A "SIDEWAYS" FORCE — PERPENDICULAR TO BOTH THE FIELD LINE AND THE CHARGE'S VELOCITY:

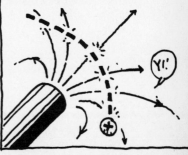

F

V

FIELD

N

153

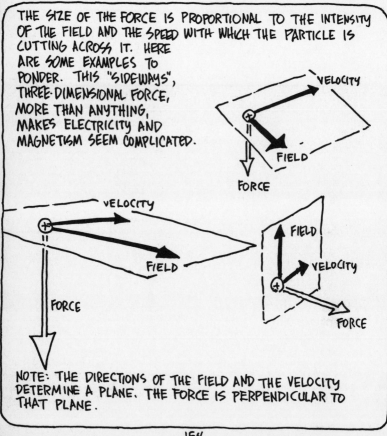

THE SIZE OF THE FORCE IS PROPORTIONAL TO THE INTENSITY OF THE FIELD AND THE SPEED WITH WHICH THE PARTICLE IS CUTTING ACROSS IT. HERE ARE SOME EXAMPLES TO PONDER. THIS "SIDEWAYS", THREE-DIMENSIONAL FORCE, MORE THAN ANYTHING, MAKES ELECTRICITY AND MAGNETISM SEEM COMPLICATED.

NOTE: THE DIRECTIONS OF THE FIELD AND THE VELOCITY DETERMINE A PLANE. THE FORCE IS PERPENDICULAR TO THAT PLANE.

HERE IS A MAGNETIC FIELD
THAT WILL MAKE CHARGED
PARTICLES CIRCLE
INDEFINITELY BETWEEN
TWO NEARBY OPPOSITE
POLE FACES:

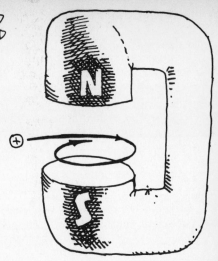

THE MAGNETIC FIELD BETWEEN THE FACES IS ALWAYS
PERPENDICULAR TO THE PARTICLE'S VELOCITY: SO THE

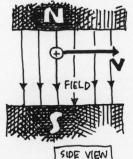

SIDE VIEW

FORCE,
PERPENDICULAR
TO BOTH,
POINTS
TO THE
CENTER
OF THE
CIRCLE!

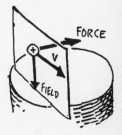

FORCE

THIS PROVIDES JUST THE
CENTRIPETAL FORCE
NEEDED TO KEEP THE
PARTICLE IN CIRCULAR
MOTION! SEEN FROM
ABOVE, IT LOOKS LIKE
THIS FAMILIAR PICTURE:

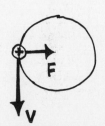

THIS IS THE BASIS
FOR THE LARGE
PARTICLE
ACCELERATORS AND
STORAGE RINGS.

MAGNETS EXERT FORCES ON
MOVING PARTICLES — AND,
AS OERSTED SHOWED,
MOVING CHARGES ALSO
CREATE MAGNETIC FIELDS.
THAT'S WHAT DEFLECTED
OERSTED'S COMPASS...

IT'S THE GREATEST DISCOVERY SINCE THE PRUNE DANISH!

TO EXAMINE THE SIMPLEST CASE, LET US PASS A CURRENT-
CARRYING WIRE STRAIGHT THROUGH A PLANE COVERED WITH
COMPASS NEEDLES:

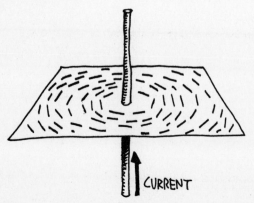

CURRENT

THE NEEDLES LINE UP IN CIRCLES AROUND THE WIRE.

THE MAGNETIC
FIELD OF A CURRENT
IS CIRCLES CENTERED
ON THE WIRE AND
LYING IN THE PLANE
PERPENDICULAR
TO THE CURRENT.

FIELD CURRENT

YOU CAN FIND THE DIRECTION OF THE MAGNETIC FIELD BY POINTING THE THUMB OF YOUR RIGHT HAND ALONG THE DIRECTION OF THE FLOW OF POSITIVE CHARGES. YOUR FINGERS CURL IN THE DIRECTION OF THE MAGNETIC FIELD.

THIS IS KNOWN AS THE

right-hand rule.

DYSLEXIC ELECTRICIANS ARE RARE...

MEDIUM RARE IF THEY'RE NOT CAREFUL!

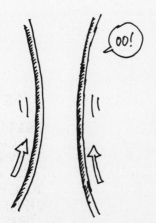

OO!

TWO PARALLEL CURRENTS ATTRACT EACH OTHER. THE MAGNETIC FIELD CIRCLING EACH WIRE CAUSE FORCES ON THE CURRENT IN THE OTHER WIRE, PULLING IT CLOSER.
SEE IF YOU CAN CONVINCE YOURSELF THAT THIS IS THE RIGHT DIRECTION, USING THE RIGHT-HAND RULE!

AMPERE, DISCOVERER OF THE FORCE BETWEEN PARALLEL WIRES

1775   1836

IF WE BEND A CURRENT-CARRYING WIRE INTO A CIRCLE, WE GET THIS MAGNETIC FIELD:

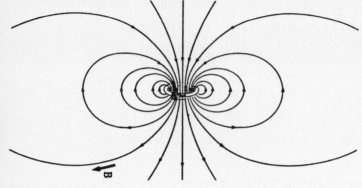

NOTICE THAT ONE SIDE LOOKS JUST LIKE A **NORTH** POLE — THE FIELD LINES ARE COMING OUT. — AND THE OTHER SIDE LOOKS LIKE A **SOUTH** POLE, WITH FIELD LINES GOING IN...

WHOA!

BY WINDING MANY TURNS, THE MAGNETIC FIELD IS MADE PROPORTIONALLY LARGER. BY WINDING TURNS ALONG A CYLINDER, WE GET A **SOLENOID COIL**, WITH A MAGNETIC FIELD JUST LIKE A BAR MAGNET!

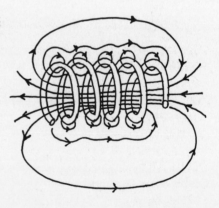

COME HERE OFTEN?

INSERTING AN IRON BAR INTO THE COIL CONCENTRATES AND STRENGTHENS THE MAGNETIC FIELD, AND THE RESULT IS AN

ELECTRO-MAGNET.

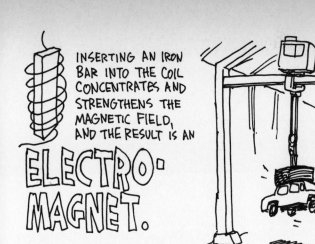

MAYBE YOU'RE GETTING CONFUSED WITH ALL THESE MAGNETIC AND ELECTRIC FIELDS. SUPPOSE THE ROOM WERE FILLED WITH THEM — HOW WOULD YOU KNOW, AND HOW WOULD YOU KNOW WHICH WAS WHICH?

IN FACT, THE ROOM **IS** FILLED WITH THEM. THERE'S THE EARTH'S MAGNETIC FIELD, AND THE ELECTRIC AND MAGNETIC FIELDS OF RADIO WAVES THAT YOU CAN PICK UP WITH AN ANTENNA. (THE ELECTRIC FIELD OF RADIO WAVES MOVES THE CHARGES IN THE ANTENNA.) YOU CAN TEST FOR MAGNETIC FIELDS WITH A COMPASS, OR BY STUDYING THE SIDEWAYS FORCES ON MOVING CHARGES.

THIS CAN'T BE HEALTHY...

159

·CHAPTER 18·
PERMANENT MAGNETS

ALL KNOWN
MAGNETIC FIELDS
RESULT FROM
MOVING ELECTRIC
CHARGES.

ALL?

WHERE ARE THE CHARGES THAT CREATE THE MAGNETIC FIELD OF AN IRON MAGNET? THEY ARE THE ELECTRONS IN THE IRON ATOMS THEMSELVES!

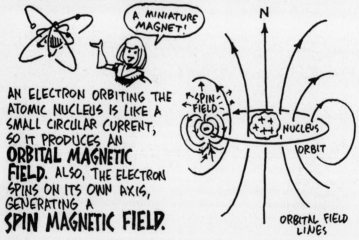

A MINIATURE MAGNET!

AN ELECTRON ORBITING THE ATOMIC NUCLEUS IS LIKE A SMALL CIRCULAR CURRENT, SO IT PRODUCES AN **ORBITAL MAGNETIC FIELD.** ALSO, THE ELECTRON SPINS ON ITS OWN AXIS, GENERATING A **SPIN MAGNETIC FIELD.**

N

SPIN FIELD

NUCLEUS

ORBIT

ORBITAL FIELD LINES

MOST ELECTRONS IN
ATOMS HAVE THEIR
MAGNETIC FIELDS
CANCELLED OUT BY
THE MAGNETIC FIELDS
OF OTHER ELECTRONS...

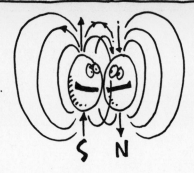

BUT IN **MAGNETIC** MATERIALS — LIKE THE METALS **IRON, NICKEL,** AND **COBALT** — THERE ARE LONE ELECTRONS THAT CONTRIBUTE A NET MAGNETIC FIELD TO EACH ATOM.

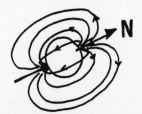

... AND
FURTHERMORE,

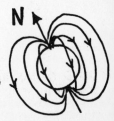

IN THESE "FERROMAGNETIC" ELEMENTS, THE ATOMS THEMSELVES LINE UP SO THAT THEIR MAGNETIC FIELDS ALL POINT IN THE SAME DIRECTION. RESULT: A BIG MAGNETIC FIELD!

ELECTRONIC
FASCISM!

BUT IF ALL THE ATOMS ARE LINED UP, WHY AREN'T ALL PIECES OF IRON MAGNETIC?

ALL THE ATOMS IN MICROSCOPIC REGIONS OF THE MATERIAL, CALLED **DOMAINS**, DO LINE UP, BUT IN UNMAGNETIZED IRON, THE DOMAINS ARE RANDOMLY ORIENTED. WHEN THE IRON IS PLACED IN A MAGNETIC FIELD, THE DOMAINS TEND TO LINE UP WITH THE FIELD, AND THE IRON BECOMES MAGNETIZED.

UNMAGNETIZED

MAGNETIZED

SOME METAL ALLOYS ARE MAGNETICALLY "HARD." IT TAKES A STRONG EXTERNAL MAGNETIC FIELD TO ORIENT THEIR DOMAINS— BUT ONCE ORIENTED, THE DOMAINS TEND TO STAY LINED UP.

ALNICO V,

AN ALLOY OF ALUMINUM, NICKEL, COBALT, IRON, AND COPPER, IS VERY MAGNETICALLY HARD. PURE IRON, ON THE OTHER HAND IS MAGNETICALLY "SOFT": EASILY MAGNETIZED, BUT EASILY DEMAGNETIZED BY REMOVING THE EXTERNAL FIELD.

BONG BONG

CAN'T SHAKE IT!

THE FERROMAGNETIC EFFECT OPERATES ONLY BELOW A CRITICAL TEMPERATURE, 770°C FOR IRON. HEATING DISRUPTS MAGNETISM.

SST! WANNA BUY A "HOT" MAGNET?

CERTAINLY NOT.

PRESUMABLY, THE EARTH'S MAGNETISM IS CAUSED BY CIRCULATING ELECTRIC FIELDS IN THE EARTH'S CORE. THE EXACT MECHANISM REMAINS A MYSTERY. DO YOU FIND IT RATHER AMUSING THAT THE FIRST MAGNETIC EFFECTS EVER DISCOVERED ARE STILL NOT SATISFACTORILY EXPLAINED?

HA HA HA HA HA HA HA

·CHAPTER 19·
FARADAY INDUCTION

FOR TWELVE YEARS AFTER
OERSTED'S DISCOVERY,
"ELECTRICIANS" LOOKED
FOR THE COMPLEMENTARY
EFFECT: HOW TO MAKE
A MAGNETIC FIELD PRODUCE
A CURRENT? AT LAST, IN
1832, MICHAEL FARADAY
MADE A SUGGESTION—

MOVE THE
MAGNET!

HERE RINGO THRUSTS A MAGNET INTO A LOOP OF WIRE CONNECTED TO A SENSITIVE CURRENT METER, A GALVANOMETER. THE GALVANO-METER NEEDLE DEFLECTS!

WHEN THE MAGNET IS HELD STILL, THE METER REGISTERS NO CURRENT.

STEADY...

ANOTHER WAY TO INDUCE CURRENT IS TO PLACE A SECOND LOOP NEARBY AND ENERGIZE IT WITH A BATTERY. WHEN CURRENT IN THE SECOND LOOP IS SWITCHED ON OR OFF, A CURRENT PULSE IS INDUCED IN THE FIRST!

SWITCH

BATTERY

BUT WHEN THE CURRENT IN THE SECOND LOOP IS STEADY, NO CURRENT IS INDUCED IN THE FIRST LOOP.

CURRENT FLOWS IN 2. BUT NOT IN 1.

1.

2.

ISN'T IT MIRACULOUS, ENERGY INVISIBLY GETTING ACROSS SPACE ??

NOT IF YOU BELIEVE IN FIELDS, IT ISN'T...

FARADAY DESCRIBED THIS BY SAYING THAT **ELECTRO-MOTIVE FORCES** ARE GENERATED IN THE WIRE WHENEVER MAGNETIC FIELD LINES CUT ACROSS THE WIRE.

EMF FOR SHORT!

165

IT DOESN'T MATTER WHETHER THE MAGNETIC FIELD MOVES OR THE WIRE MOVES WITH RESPECT TO THE MAGNET.

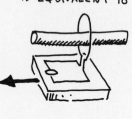

IS EQUIVALENT TO

IGNORANT WIRE CAN'T TELL THE DIFFERENCE!

WHEN THE MAGNET IS THRUST INTO THE LOOP, ITS FIELD LINES CUT ACROSS THE WIRE, GENERATING AN **EMF** THAT PRODUCES A CURRENT.

DITTO WHEN THE LOOP IS MOVED OVER THE MAGNET.

IN THE CASE OF TWO WIRE LOOPS, WHEN CURRENT IS FIRST TURNED ON IN ONE LOOP, MAGNETIC FIELD LINES BUILD UP, CUTTING ACROSS THE OTHER LOOP AND PRODUCING AN EMF.

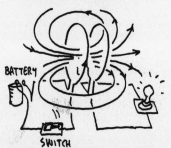

BATTERY

SWITCH

WHEN THE CURRENT IS SWITCHED OFF, THE FIELD LINES COLLAPSE, AGAIN CUTTING ACROSS THE LOOP.

TWELVE YEARS TO MOVE THE MAGNET?

A MILDLY AMUSING BUT HARDLY USEFUL RESULT...

YESS... NOW LET'S GET ON WITH THE REALLY IMPORTANT RESEARCH... HOW LUMPS IN THE SKULL AFFECT CRIMINAL TENDENCIES...

LA PHRENOLOGIE

ALTHOUGH FARADAY'S DISCOVERY WAS AT FIRST RECEIVED WITH INDIFFERENCE, TODAY ALL OUR ELECTRIC POWER IS GENERATED BY MOVING GIANT COILS OF WIRE NEAR MAGNETS!

IT IS ASTONISHING THAT JUST BY ARRANGING COPPER AND STEEL IN A HYDROELECTRIC PLANT, FALLING WATER CAN ROTATE TURBINES WHICH GENERATE ENOUGH ELECTRICITY TO POWER CITIES HUNDREDS OF MILES AWAY!!

167

LET'S STUDY FARADAY'S EXPERIMENT FURTHER. WHEN WE MOVE THE MAGNET NEAR THE LOOP, GENERATING CURRENT, WHERE DOES THE **ENERGY** COME FROM TO MOVE THE GALVANOMETER NEEDLE?

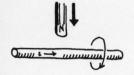

WHEN THE INDUCED CURRENT FLOWS IN THE WIRE, IT MAKES A MAGNETIC FIELD. THIS MAGNETIC FIELD MUST RESIST THE MAGNET'S MOTION, SO WORK IS DONE IN MOVING IT.

WHEN RINGO THRUSTS THE NORTH POLE OF THE MAGNET INTO THE LOOP, THE CURRENT MUST FLOW IN A DIRECTION TO MAKE A NORTH POLE REPELLING THE MAGNET.

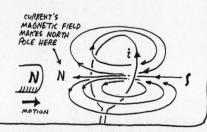

CURRENT'S MAGNETIC FIELD MAKES NORTH POLE HERE

MOTION

THIS IS KNOWN AS **LENZ'S LAW:** INDUCED CURRENT FLOWS IN A DIRECTION TO OPPOSE THE CHANGE THAT PRODUCED IT.

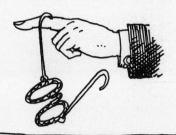

LENZ'S LAW IS A CONSEQUENCE OF ENERGY CONSERVATION. A USEFUL APPLICATION IS THE **MAGNETIC BRAKE** USED IN TROLLEYS. AN ELECTROMAGNET IS PLACED NEAR THE TRACK. THEN THE CURRENT IN THE ELECTROMAGNET INDUCES AN OPPOSING CURRENT IN THE TRACK, SLOWING THE TROLLEY.

· CHAPTER 20 ·
RELATIVITY

LET'S THINK THROUGH THE FARADAY EXPERIMENT AGAIN. I HOLD THE LOOP, RINGO THE MAGNET. WHEN I MOVE, SO DOES THE GALVANOMETER NEEDLE.

THIS IS EASILY UNDERSTOOD. THE WIRE HAS CHARGES. WHEN THEY MOVE, THEY FEEL THE SIDEWAYS MAGNETIC FORCE WHICH DRIVES THEM AROUND THE LOOP.

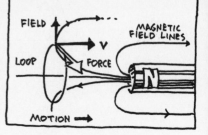

FIELD

LOOP

MOTION →

V

FORCE

N

MAGNETIC FIELD LINES

BUT WHAT ABOUT WHEN RINGO MOVES AND I STAND STILL?

UM, AH, ER, EH, DUH..

WE KNOW THAT A CURRENT IS INDUCED, BUT BY WHAT? THE CHARGES ARE NOT INITIALLY MOVING, SO HOW CAN THE MAGNET AFFECT THEM?

IF ONLY MAGNETIC AND ELECTRIC FIELDS CAN MOVE CHARGES, THERE MUST HAVE BEEN AN ELECTRIC FIELD, TOO?

BRAVO!

RINGO HAS DEDUCED WHAT IT TOOK EINSTEIN TO REALIZE. EINSTEIN SAW THAT, DEPENDING ON WHO WAS MOVING, THE CURRENT IS SOMETIMES DUE TO A MAGNETIC FIELD AND SOMETIMES TO AN ELECTRIC FIELD.

CHANGING MAGNETIC FIELDS CAUSE ELECTRIC FIELDS !!

NOW AGAIN... ONE MORE TIME... WE'LL DO THE FARADAY EXPERIMENT...
BUT THIS TIME IN **OUTER SPACE**, SO WE CAN'T TELL WHO IS
"REALLY" MOVING. WE KNOW ONLY THAT WE ARE MOVING
RELATIVE TO EACH OTHER.

I THINK I AM STATIONARY, AND RINGO IS MOVING. I DETECT A MAGNETIC FIELD, BUT IT CAN'T MOVE THE CHARGES, SO THERE MUST BE AN ELECTRIC FIELD ALSO, CAUSED BY THE CHANGING MAGNETIC FIELD.

RINGO THINKS HE IS STATIONARY AND I AM MOVING. HE DETECTS ONLY A MAGNETIC FIELD AND MOVING CHARGES, WHICH ACCOUNT FOR THE INDUCED CURRENT.

LUCY SEES TWO FIELDS

RINGO SEES ONLY A MAGNETIC FIELD

RINGO AND I DISAGREE ON WHAT FIELDS ARE PRESENT!

AND DOT'S RELATIVITY!

THIS IS THE HALLMARK OF RELATIVITY THEORY: TWO OBSERVERS LIKE RINGO AND ME, IF THEY ARE MOVING WITH RESPECT TO EACH OTHER, WILL DISAGREE ON THEIR MEASUREMENTS OF KEY PHYSICAL QUANTITIES OF THE UNIVERSE!

OH, I SAY ELECTRIC, AND YOU SAY MAGNETIC..

HERE'S AN EVEN SIMPLER ILLUSTRATION: A SINGLE CHARGE ZIPS THROUGH SPACE PAST RINGO:

RINGO SEES A MOVING CHARGE — A CURRENT THAT GENERATES A MAGNETIC FIELD. THE NEEDLE OF RINGO'S COMPASS DEFLECTS!

BUT IF I AM MOVING WITH THE CHARGE, I SEE IT AS STATIONARY. THERE IS NO MAGNETIC FIELD, AND MY COMPASS IS NOT AFFECTED!

BYEE!

HERE'S THE FINAL DEMONSTRATION: WATCH CAREFULLY! I NOW CARRY **TWO** CHARGES SIDE BY SIDE PAST RINGO.

THEY REPEL EACH OTHER ELECTRICALLY — BUT RINGO SEES THEM MOVING: TWO PARALLEL CURRENTS, WHICH ATTRACT MAGNETICALLY!

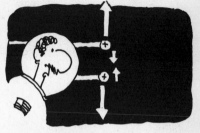

BUT TO ME, THE CHARGES ARE STATIONARY, SO I SEE ONLY THE REPULSION.

NOW I LET GO OF THE CHARGES. THEY FLY APART.

NOW THE STRANGE PART: RINGO SEES AN ATTRACTIVE MAGNETIC FORCE BETWEEN THE CHARGES, WHICH PARTLY OFFSETS THE REPULSIVE ELECTRIC FORCE — SO RINGO SEES THE CHARGES MOVE APART MORE SLOWLY THAN I DO!

GOT THAT? RINGO, WHO IS MOVING WITH RESPECT TO ME, MEASURES THE CHARGES' OUTWARD VELOCITY TO BE **SLOWER** THAN I MEASURE IT!!

YUP. DOT'S RELATIVITY!

HERE IS AN APPARATUS FOR MEASURING HOW FAST THE CHARGES FLY APART.

PULLING TRIGGER **A** RELEASES BLOCKS **B**, STARTING CLOCK **C** AND ALLOWING CHARGES **Q** TO FLY APART. CHARGES STRIKE CUPS **D**, STOPPING CLOCK **C**.

WITH THE THING AT REST IN FRONT OF ME, THE CHARGES FLY APART QUICKLY, SAY IN 0.01 SECONDS.

BUT, AS WE JUST SAW, THE SPEEDING RINGO SEES A MAGNETIC ATTRACTION THAT DELAYS THE CHARGES' FLYING APART.

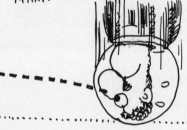

RINGO MEASURES A **LONGER TIME** THAN I DO—SAY 0.02 SEC., FOR THE CHARGES TO FLY APART! HE ALSO NOTICES THAT MY CLOCK TICKS OFF ONLY 0.01 SEC. IN THE TIME IT TOOK HIS CLOCK TO REACH 0.02 SECONDS. CONCLUSION?

174

WHAT IS RINGO TO THINK?
AS I SPEED BY, HE SEES MY
CLOCK TICK OFF 0.01 SECONDS,
WHILE HIS TICKS OFF TWICE AS
MUCH. THERE IS ONLY ONE
THING HE CAN CONCLUDE.
RINGO DECIDES THAT—

MY RAPID MOTION CAUSED MY TIME TO SLOW DOWN!!

EITHER THAT, OR MY SPACESUIT HAS SPRUNG A LEAK...

THAT IS JUST ONE OF THE WEIRD CONCLUSIONS OF RELATIVITY THEORY. AND THERE ARE MORE. ACCORDING TO EINSTEIN, A STATIONARY OBSERVER SEES THE FOLLOWING EFFECTS ON RAPIDLY MOVING OBJECTS:

* **TIME SLOWS DOWN**

* **LENGTHS DECREASE**
  (IN THE DIRECTION OF MOTION)

* **MASSES INCREASE**

IN OTHER WORDS—

SOME OF OUR MOST CHERISHED IDEAS ABOUT SPACE AND TIME ARE RELATIVE, NOT ABSOLUTE!

175

WE SAW THAT THE EFFECT OF TIME DILATION IS DERIVED FROM BASIC, OBSERVED FACTS ABOUT ELECTRICITY AND MAGNETISM. THE PHYSICISTS OF THE LATE NINETEENTH CENTURY ALREADY KNEW THAT THEIR E.M. EQUATIONS DID NOT AGREE WITH NEWTON'S MECHANICS, AND MOST OF THEM THOUGHT THE ANSWER WAS TO MODIFY THE EQUATIONS IN SOME WAY...

...BUT ONLY EINSTEIN SAW THAT THE ANSWER WAS TO REVISE THE VERY CONCEPTS OF SPACE AND TIME...

·CHAPTER 21·
INDUCTORS

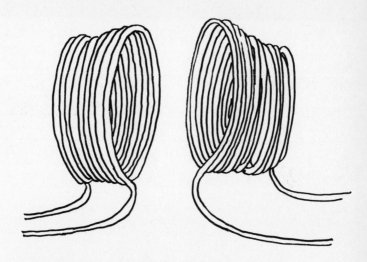

AN INDUCTOR IS SIMPLY A COIL OF WIRE.
SOMETIMES IT MAY SURROUND AN IRON CORE,
TO INCREASE MAGNETIC EFFECTS. ITS
ELECTRIC SYMBOL IS:

INDUCTOR **L**

INDUCTOR **L** WITH
IRON CORE.

IF A CURRENT FLOWS THROUGH AN INDUCTOR, A MAGNETIC FIELD WILL SURROUND IT, AS WE'VE SEEN.

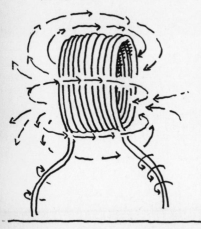

IF THE CURRENT IS CHANGED, MAGNETIC FIELD LINES CUT ACROSS THE TURNS OF THE COIL, PRODUCING A **SELF-INDUCTANCE** EFFECT.

TWO NEIGHBORING TURNS!

BY LENZ'S LAW, THE INDUCED EMF OPPOSES THE CHANGE THAT PRODUCED IT. IF YOU TRY TO TURN ON THE CURRENT IN THE COIL, THE SELF-INDUCED EMF RESISTS, AND THE CURRENT CAN ONLY BUILD UP SLOWLY. IF YOU TRY TO TURN IT OFF, THE SELF-INDUCED EMF TRIES TO KEEP THE CURRENT FLOWING.

IT'S LIKE INERTIA!

THESE EMFs CAN BUILD UP TO THOUSANDS OF VOLTS. FOR EXAMPLE, WHEN YOU OPEN A SWITCH, THIS EMF CAN SHOOT A SPARK THROUGH THE AIR, KEEPING THE CURRENT FLOWING FOR A MOMENT.

ZAP

THE EFFECT IS EXPLOITED IN THE IGNITION CIRCUIT OF AN AUTOMOBILE.

I SUPPOSE THERE'S SOME USE FOR THIS CHARMING PHENOMENON?

EMF 1

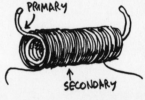

THE "COIL" HAS TWO WINDINGS, A PRIMARY WINDING OF, SAY, A HUNDRED TURNS OF MEDIUM-SIZED WIRE, AND A SECONDARY WINDING OF THOUSANDS OF TURNS OF FINE WIRE. THE PRIMARY IS ENERGIZED THROUGH THE "POINTS"* BY THE 12-VOLT BATTERY. WHEN THE POINTS OPEN, SWITCHING OFF THE CURRENT IN THE PRIMARY, THE COLLAPSING MAGNETIC FIELD INDUCES CURRENT IN THE SECONDARY. THE MANY TURNS AMPLIFY THE INDUCED EMF, AND GENERATE A MOMENTARY PULSE OF NEARLY

50,000 VOLTS!!

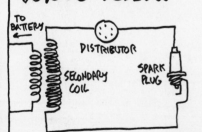

TO BATTERY

DISTRIBUTOR

SECONDARY COIL

SPARK PLUG

THIS IS DIRECTED BY THE DISTRIBUTOR TO THE SPARK PLUGS, PRODUCING A SPARK WHICH IGNITES THE GASOLINE. IN THIS WAY, A 12-VOLT BATTERY IS AMPLIFIED TO A HIGH-VOLTAGE SPARK.

*MODERN IGNITION SYSTEMS USE ELECTRONIC SWITCHES.

⁞CHAPTER 22⁞
AC AND DC

SO FAR WE'VE BEEN LOOKING ONLY AT **DC** — DIRECT CURRENT: A FLOW OF CHARGE IN ONE DIRECTION DOWN A WIRE.

BUT WE USUALLY USE **AC** — ALTERNATING CURRENT, IN WHICH THE FLOW IS CONSTANTLY CHANGING DIRECTION. IN YOUR HOUSE WIRING, WHICH IS AC, IT REVERSES DIRECTION 120 TIMES EVERY SECOND!

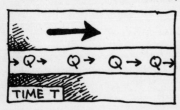

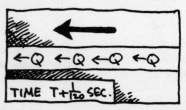

I CAN GENERATE AN ALTERNATING CURRENT BY SPINNING THIS EGGBEATER-LIKE INDUCTOR IN A PERMANENT MAGNETIC FIELD. IT DEVELOPS A CURRENT AS IT CUTS ACROSS THE MAGNETIC FIELD LINES.

THE CURRENT ALTERNATES BECAUSE THE LOOP CUTS THE FIELD LINES FIRST ONE WAY...

..AND THEN THE OTHER, A HALF TURN LATER.

THE AC THUS GENERATED CAN BE TAKEN OFF BY SLIP RING "BRUSHES." THIS IS HOW MOST OF OUR ELECTRIC POWER IS GENERATED.

WOW. YOU ARE WOMAN. YOU ARE STRONG.

SLIP RINGS

181

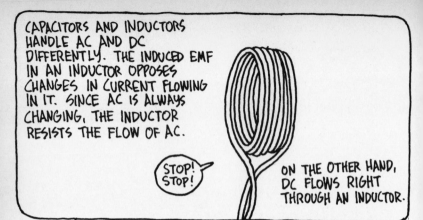

CAPACITORS AND INDUCTORS HANDLE AC AND DC DIFFERENTLY. THE INDUCED EMF IN AN INDUCTOR OPPOSES CHANGES IN CURRENT FLOWING IN IT. SINCE AC IS ALWAYS CHANGING, THE INDUCTOR RESISTS THE FLOW OF AC.

STOP! STOP!

ON THE OTHER HAND, DC FLOWS RIGHT THROUGH AN INDUCTOR.

DC, OF COURSE, WON'T FLOW THROUGH A CAPACITOR—THERE IS NO CONNECTION BETWEEN THE CAPACITOR PLATES. BUT AC CAN "GET THROUGH" A CAPACITOR!

PRESTO!

IT WORKS LIKE THIS: CHARGE MOVES BACK AND FORTH IN THE CIRCUIT, ALTERNATELY CHARGING A PLATE, DISCHARGING IT, AND RECHARGING IT THE OPPOSITE WAY. THE CURRENT APPEARS TO CROSS THE GAP.

1.　　　　2.　　　　3.

182

AN INDUCTOR'S
RESISTANCE TO
AC GIVES IT A
KIND OF INERTIA.
IN FACT, AN
INDUCTOR IS AN
ELECTRICAL
ANALOG OF A
MASS.

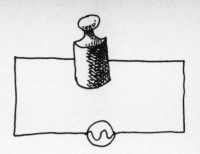

IF AN INDUCTOR IS MASSLIKE, A CAPACITOR IS SPRINGY.
WHEN YOU TRY TO PUMP CHARGE TO AN ALREADY CHARGED
PLATE, IT PUSHES BACK—LIKE A SPRING.

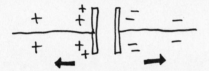

CAPACITOR
REPELS ADDED
CHARGE

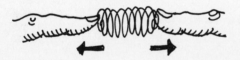

SPRING REPELS
ADDED PRESSURE

CONNECT AN
INDUCTOR AND A
CAPACITOR IN AN
AC CIRCUIT, AND
YOU HAVE THE
ELECTRICAL EQUIVALENT
OF—A MASS
ON A SPRING!

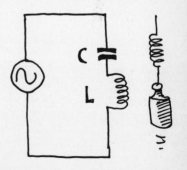

183

LIKE A SPRING AND MASS, THESE
LC CIRCUITS TEND TO VIBRATE
AT A PREFERRED ("RESONANT") FREQUENCY.

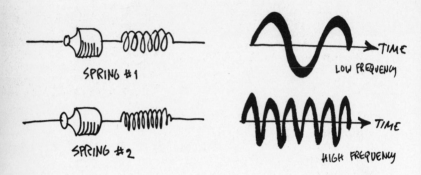

SPRING #1

SPRING #2

TIME
LOW FREQUENCY

TIME
HIGH FREQUENCY

SUCH A CIRCUIT CAN
BE USED (WITH AN ENERGY
SOURCE) TO GENERATE A
SPECIFIC FREQUENCY, OR
TO TUNE ONE IN, AS
IN YOUR RADIO.

HELLO, AND WELCOME
TO ANOTHER BORING
PROGRAM FROM
AN OBSOLETE
MEDIUM...

BECAUSE! RECALL THE TWO INDUCTION COILS FROM THE FARADAY EXPERIMENT (OR FROM YOUR CAR STARTER). CURRENT WAS INDUCED IN COIL #2 ONLY WHEN THE CURRENT TO COIL #1 WAS TURNED ON OR OFF. ONLY CHANGING CURRENT CAN INDUCE CURRENT.

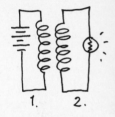

1. 2.

BUT AC CURRENT IS ALWAYS CHANGING.

I GET IT: AC ALWAYS INDUCES CURRENT. SO WHAT?

THE BEST PART IS THIS: THE INDUCED VOLTAGE IS PROPORTIONAL TO THE

TURNS RATIO:

THE MORE TURNS IN COIL #2 AS COMPARED TO COIL #1, THE HIGHER THE VOLTAGE INDUCED IN COIL #2!

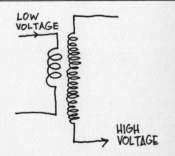

LOW VOLTAGE

HIGH VOLTAGE

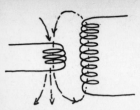

IT IS NOT HARD TO SEE WHY: IN THE SECONDARY, THE MORE WIRE IS CUT BY THE CHANGING MAGNETIC FIELD LINES, THE MORE EMF IS GENERATED. IF

N_P = NUMBER OF TURNS IN PRIMARY

N_S = NUMBER OF TURNS IN SECONDARY

THEN

$$V_{OUT} = \frac{N_S}{N_P} V_{IN}$$

STEPPING UP VOLTAGE

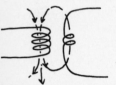

STEPPING DOWN VOLTAGE

THE RESULTING DEVICE, FOR STEPPING VOLTAGE UP OR DOWN, IS CALLED A

TRANSFORMER

WITH THE SYMBOL

AND IT WORKS ONLY FOR **AC**.

LOOKS LIKE VOLTAGE FROM NOWHERE?

A TRANSFORMER "TRANSFORMS" VOLTAGES UP OR DOWN — AND NO, YOU CAN'T GET SOMETHING FOR NOTHING. THE **POWER** OUTPUT OF THE SECONDARY COIL CAN NOT EXCEED THE POWER INPUT OF THE PRIMARY. IN OTHER WORDS, AS YOU STEP UP THE VOLTAGE, YOU MUST STEP DOWN THE CURRENT.

$$P_{OUT} = V_{OUT} i_{OUT} \leq P_{IN} = V_{IN} i_{IN}$$

CONSERVATION OF ENERGY? YOU BET!

THIS, THEN, IS THE GREAT ADVANTAGE OF ALTERNATING CURRENT: ITS VOLTAGE CAN BE EASILY STEPPED UP OR DOWN.

THIS IS ESPECIALLY IMPORTANT BETWEEN POWER GENERATING STATIONS AND THE CUSTOMERS THEY SERVE:

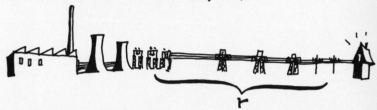

THE TRANSMISSION WIRES HAVE A RESISTANCE r, SO THERE IS A VOLTAGE DROP $V = ir$ AND POWER LOSS $P = iV = i^2 r$ ALONG THE LINE. AT HIGH CURRENT i, ENORMOUS AMOUNTS OF POWER ARE WASTED.

THAT'S WHERE TRANSFORMERS COME IN!

BY STEPPING UP TO VERY HIGH VOLTAGE (MORE THAN 100,000 VOLTS!) AT THE SOURCE, CURRENT IS REDUCED IN THE WIRES, AND THE POWER LOSS IS MINIMIZED. THEN, AT THE USER'S END, VOLTAGE IS STEPPED DOWN TO A RELATIVELY SAFE 220 OR 110 VOLTS.

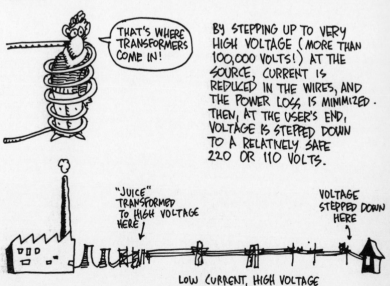

"JUICE" TRANSFORMED TO HIGH VOLTAGE HERE

VOLTAGE STEPPED DOWN HERE

LOW CURRENT, HIGH VOLTAGE

187

OUR HUGE ELECTRIC
POWER SYSTEM IS
ALL DUE TO THE
HUMBLE TRANSFORMER.

WITH THE INVENTION OF HIGH-TEMPERATURE
SUPERCONDUCTORS
AND HIGH-TECH DEVICES FOR TRANSFORMING
DC VOLTAGES, WE MAY SEE SOME
DC POWER LINES IN COMING DECADES.

CHAPTER 23

MAXWELL'S EQUATIONS AND LIGHT (AND HOW!)

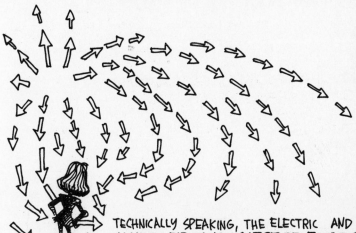

TECHNICALLY SPEAKING, THE ELECTRIC AND MAGNETIC FIELDS ARE **VECTOR FIELDS** — FIELDS WITH A MAGNITUDE AND DIRECTION AT EVERY POINT. TO DESCRIBE A VECTOR FIELD, YOU MUST SPECIFY HOW THE FIELD SPREADS OUT, OR **DIVERGES,** AND HOW IT CIRCLES AROUND, OR **CURLS.** (DIVERGENCE AND CURL ARE MATHEMATICAL TERMS.)

IN 1873, JAMES CLERK

MAXWELL

WROTE DOWN FOUR EQUATIONS WHICH SPECIFY THE CURL AND DIVERGENCE OF THE ELECTRIC AND MAGNETIC FIELDS.

Maxwell 1831 - 1879

MAXWELL'S FIRST EQUATION IS GAUSS'S LAW. IT SAYS THAT ELECTRIC FIELD LINES **DIVERGE** FROM POSITIVE CHARGES AND **CONVERGE** TO NEGATIVE CHARGES.

THE SECOND EQUATION IS FARADAY'S LAW: ELECTRIC FIELD LINES **CURL** AROUND CHANGING MAGNETIC FIELDS. CHANGING MAGNETIC FIELDS INDUCE ELECTRIC FIELDS.

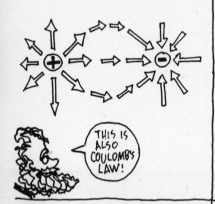

THIS IS ALSO COULOMB'S LAW!

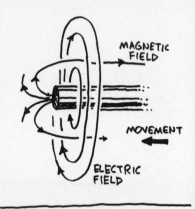

MAGNETIC FIELD

MOVEMENT

ELECTRIC FIELD

THE THIRD EQUATION SAYS THAT MAGNETIC FIELDS NEVER DIVERGE OR CONVERGE. THEY ALWAYS GO IN CLOSED CURVES.

FINALLY, THE LAST EQUATION SAYS THAT MAGNETIC FIELD LINES **CURL** AROUND ELECTRIC CURRENTS. WE HAVE SEEN THAT A MAGNETIC FIELD CIRCLES AROUND A CONDUCTING WIRE.

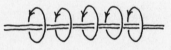

THROUGH THE MAGNET!

N   S

...AND HERE MAXWELL HAD A CRITICAL BRAINSTORM! (AN ELECTRICAL STORM, OF COURSE!)

190

AS YOU SEE, THE EQUATIONS EXPRESS LAWS THAT CAME TO MAXWELL FROM OTHER SOURCES. BUT MAXWELL'S GENIUS WAS TO SEE THAT LAW #4 WAS INCOMPLETE.

I JUST HAD THIS FEELING!

CONSIDER A CAPACITOR BEING CHARGED. AS THE CURRENT FLOWS TO THE CAPACITOR PLATES, A MAGNETIC FIELD RINGS THE WIRE. BUT WHAT ABOUT BETWEEN THE PLATES?

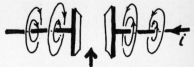

NO MAGNETIC FIELD HERE?

DOES THE FIELD STOP ABRUPTLY BETWEEN THE PLATES, WHERE THE CURRENT STOPS? MAXWELL SAID—

IN A WORD, HUH-UH.

MAXWELL FELT THAT NATURE DISLIKES DISCONTINUITIES. ALSO, HE REASONED THAT IF CHANGING MAGNETIC FIELDS INDUCE ELECTRIC FIELDS (FARADAY), THEN, SYMMETRICALLY, CHANGING ELECTRIC FIELDS MIGHT INDUCE MAGNETIC FIELDS. THERE WAS NO EVIDENCE FOR THIS, OF COURSE, BUT...

HEY, LET'S CHECK IT OUT...

THUS, MAXWELL ADDED AN EXTRA TERM TO HIS FOURTH EQUATION, SAYING THAT MAGNETIC FIELDS ALSO **CURL** AROUND CHANGING ELECTRIC FIELDS. THIS TERM GENERATES A MAGNETIC FIELD BETWEEN THE CAPACITOR PLATES AS THE ELECTRIC FIELD BUILDS UP.

SOME YEARS LATER, THIS MAGNETIC FIELD WAS DETECTED.

VICTORY!

SO, WITHOUT FURTHER ADO, HERE ARE

MAXWELL'S EQUATIONS

IN FULL-BLOWN MATHEMATICAL NOTATION
TO THRILL AND INTIMIDATE YOU!

$$\nabla \cdot E = 4\pi\rho$$ (ρ, GREEK "RHO" = CHARGE DENSITY; E = ELECTRIC FIELD) SAYS E DIVERGES OUTWARD FROM PLUS CHARGES AND INWARD TO MINUS CHARGES.

$$\nabla \times E = -\frac{1}{c}\frac{dB}{dt}$$ (B = MAGNETIC FIELD)
SAYS E CURLS AROUND CHANGING B FIELDS.
(c = SPEED OF LIGHT)

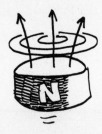

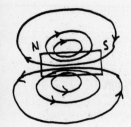

$$\nabla \cdot B = 0$$ SAYS B NEVER DIVERGES, ALWAYS LOOPS AROUND.

$$\nabla \times B = \frac{4\pi}{c}J + \frac{1}{c}\frac{dE}{dt}$$
SAYS B CURLS AROUND CURRENTS
(J = CURRENT DENSITY) AND
CHANGING E FIELDS.

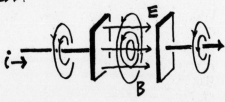

THAT ONE LITTLE TERM
ADDED TO MAXWELL'S FOURTH
EQUATION HAD AN UNEXPECTED
PAYOFF — AND A BIG ONE.

IMAGINE A SINGLE ELECTRIC CHARGE BEING **VIBRATED:** IN THE SPACE NEAR THE VIBRATING CHARGE, THE CHARGE'S ELECTRIC FIELD IS CHANGING, SO IT INDUCES A MAGNETIC FIELD CURLING AROUND IT.

BUT THE MAGNETIC FIELD IS ALSO CHANGING — SO IT INDUCES MORE ELECTRIC FIELD, WHICH INDUCES MORE MAGNETIC FIELD...

ETC.!

THE RESULT IS A
WAVE
OF FIELDS RIPPLING OUT FROM THE VIBRATING CHARGE — AT THE SPEED OF LIGHT, ACCORDING TO MAXWELL'S CALCULATIONS!

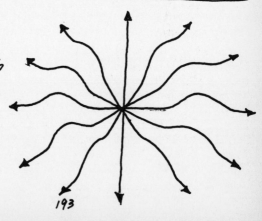

MAXWELL HAD A FLASH OF ILLUMINATION! **LIGHT** ITSELF, HE HYPOTHESIZED, IS SUCH AN **ELECTRO-MAGNETIC WAVE.**

WOW!

SOON AFTERWARD, HERTZ AND OTHERS DID INDEED PRODUCE LONG ELECTROMAGNETIC WAVES FROM WIGGLING CHARGES— AND DETECTED THEM AT A DISTANCE FROM THE SOURCE!

I'VE DISCOVERED **RADIO!!**

SIGH... AND I WAS HOPING FOR TOP 40 RADIO...

SQUEET

IT WASN'T LONG BEFORE A WHOLE SPECTRUM OF THESE WAVES WAS FOUND — FROM RADIO WAVES TO MICROWAVES TO INFRARED TO VISIBLE LIGHT TO ULTRAVIOLET TO X-RAYS AND NUCLEAR GAMMA RADIATION. IN FOUR EQUATIONS, MAXWELL NOT ONLY SUMMARIZED ELECTRICITY AND MAGNETISM, BUT ALSO ENCOMPASSED LIGHT AND OPTICS! NOT BAD!!

YEAH. THANKS, JIM!

MAX-MAN

194

·CHAPTER 24·
QUANTUM ELECTRODYNAMICS

NOW WE'RE GOING TO FIND OUT WHAT CHARGE "REALLY IS."

WEIRD. THAT'S WHAT IT IS....

WE SAW THAT ELECTROMAGNETIC THEORY ALREADY CONTAINS RELATIVITY (SEE P. 176). WHEN QUANTUM MECHANICS IS ADDED, THE THEORY BECOMES KNOWN AS

QUANTUM ELECTRO-DYNAMICS
(OR **QED**).

TELL ME ABOUT IT!

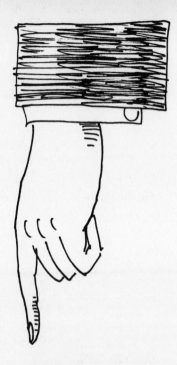

TO DISCUSS THIS, WE HAVE TO SAY A LITTLE ABOUT QUANTUM MECHANICS, THE STRANGE SYSTEM THAT PHYSICS NOW USES TO DESCRIBE THE WORLD. AMONG ITS STRANGER IDEAS ARE THESE:

* **LIGHT** IS MADE UP OF MASSLESS PARTICLES CALLED **PHOTONS**. THIS IS O.K., BECAUSE PARTICLES CAN ACT LIKE WAVES.

* NATURE IS INHERENTLY **UNCERTAIN**. IN PARTICULAR, IT IS IMPOSSIBLE TO SPECIFY A PARTICLE'S PRECISE MOMENTUM AND POSITION AT THE SAME TIME.

SO LET'S GO BACK TO THE POINT WHERE TWO POSITIVE CHARGES WERE REPELLING EACH OTHER. WE WONDERED HOW THE ELECTRIC FORCE GETS ACROSS SPACE?

QUANTUM ELECTRODYNAMICS SAYS THAT THE FORCE IS CAUSED BY PARTICLES PASSING BETWEEN THE CHARGES — PARTICLES OF LIGHT, OR **PHOTONS**. THESE PHOTONS HAVE ENERGY BUT NO MASS, AND THEY TRAVEL AT THE SPEED OF LIGHT.

PHOTON

THE STRANGE PART IS THAT THESE ARE NOT "REAL" PHOTONS LIKE THE ONES YOU SEE WITH YOUR EYES, BUT **VIRTUAL** PHOTONS — A SORT OF GHOSTLIKE PARTICLE THAT VIOLATES THE CONSERVATION OF ENERGY AND "EXISTS" FOR ONLY A LIMITED TIME.

UH·OH... IS IT WEIRD ENOUGH YET?

THE FORCE IS QUANTUM MECHANICAL IN NATURE, BUT A CLASSICAL ANALOGY IS THAT WHEN ONE CHARGE EJECTS A PHOTON, IT RECOILS SLIGHTLY. WHEN THE OTHER CHARGE CATCHES IT, IT ALSO RECOILS. THE NET EFFECT OF MANY SUCH EXCHANGES IS A REPULSIVE FORCE!

LIKE TWO PEOPLE ON ROLLER SKATES, PASSING A BASKETBALL!

WHAT ABOUT THESE "VIRTUAL" PHOTONS? EVEN A SINGLE CHARGE HAS A CLOUD OF VIRTUAL PHOTONS AROUND IT. THE CHARGE CONSTANTLY CREATES, EJECTS, AND ABSORBS VIRTUAL PHOTONS.

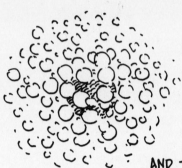

AND THIS IS THE WHOLE **QED** PICTURE (ALMOST!).

CHARGE IS JUST THE ABILITY TO MAKE VIRTUAL PHOTONS!

* * * * * * * *
AND THE ELECTRIC FIELD **IS** NOTHING BUT THE VIRTUAL PHOTON CLOUD!
* * * * * * * * *

THE STRANGEST PART OF THIS, OF COURSE, IS THAT THE VIRTUAL PHOTONS COME "FROM NOWHERE." THAT IS, AFTER A VIRTUAL PHOTON IS CREATED, THERE IS MORE TOTAL ENERGY THAN THERE WAS BEFORE IT EXISTED: THE ENERGY OF THE ORIGINAL PARTICLE PLUS THE ENERGY OF THE PHOTON.

OUTRAGEOUS!

THIS VIOLATES THE **LAW** OF CONSERVATION OF ENERGY!

LO, IS IT NOT WRITTEN?

I'M NOT CERTAIN.

THIS IS WHERE QUANTUM UNCERTAINTY COMES IN.

ONE FORM OF THE

UNCERTAINTY PRINCIPLE

IS THIS: YOU CANNOT MAKE AN EXACT DETERMINATION OF ENERGY AND TIME SIMULTANEOUSLY.

OOF!

WITHIN SHORT TIME INTERVALS, ENERGY IS "FUZZY."

THIS MEANS THAT THE ENERGY ACCOUNT CAN BE UNBALANCED —BUT ONLY FOR A TIME. A LARGE ENERGY DEFICIT MUST BE MADE UP IN A VERY SHORT TIME, WHILE A SMALL DEFICIT CAN "SIT" FOR A WHILE. (MATHEMATICALLY, $\Delta E \cdot \Delta t \geq h$: THE PRODUCT OF THE ENERGY VIOLATION TIMES THE TIME OF THE VIOLATION CAN'T BE LESS THAN A CERTAIN SMALL NUMBER h.)

DOES IT EARN INTEREST?

IN OTHER WORDS, A VERY ENERGETIC VIRTUAL PHOTON, ONE WITH A LARGE KICK, CAN'T GET FAR, EVEN AT THE SPEED OF LIGHT, BUT MUST BE REABSORBED QUICKLY TO BALANCE THE ENERGY...

GET BACK HERE!

HUP!

WOA!

HO!

WHEREAS A LOW-ENERGY PHOTON CAN TRAVEL FARTHER.

HARDLY MISS IT!

THE SMALL ENERGY VIOLATION CAN BE TOLERATED LONGER.

THIS EXPLAINS WHY THE ELECTRIC FORCE

GROWS WEAKER WITH DISTANCE!

NOT MUCH KICK OUT HERE!

PHOTONS WITH A BIG KICK CAN'T GET FAR TO DELIVER THEIR ENERGY. WHEN THE MATH IS WORKED OUT, WE GET THE FAMILIAR INVERSE-SQUARE LAW OF CLASSICAL PHYSICS. AND THERE'S NO LOWER LIMIT ON THE ENERGY OF A VIRTUAL PHOTON. A VERY LOW-ENERGY ONE CAN LAST FOR YEARS, AND TRAVEL LIGHT-YEARS. THE RANGE OF THE ELECTRIC FORCE IS UNLIMITED!

THEY CAN CROSS THE GALAXY!

THERE IS A WAY TO MAKE VIRTUAL PHOTONS REAL! HERE'S A CHARGE IN ITS CLOUD OF VIRTUAL PHOTONS:

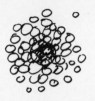

SUPPOSE WE KNOCK THE CHARGE AWAY FROM ITS VIRTUAL PHOTONS, SAY BY HITTING IT WITH ANOTHER PARTICLE.

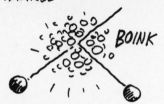

BOINK

THE VIRTUAL PHOTONS ARE ORPHANED, WITHOUT THEIR SOURCE CHARGE TO REABSORB THEM!

MOMMY!

SO THEY BECOME REAL, FLYING AWAY WITH THE ENERGY PICKED UP FROM THE COLLISION.

FLASH

IF WE SHAKE OR MOVE A CHARGE, REAL PHOTONS SHOULD COME FLYING OUT!

THIS ACTUALLY WORKS?

THIS IS HOW X·RAYS ARE MADE: SHOOT ELECTRONS INTO A HEAVY METAL, WHERE THEY ARE JERKED TO A STOP. THEIR VIRTUAL PHOTONS FLY OUT AS REAL X·RAYS.

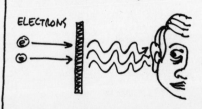

ELECTRONS

AND X-RAYS ARE REAL ENOUGH!

THEY'RE HARMLESS! REALLY!

THE PHOTONS NEEDN'T BE X-RAYS. A RADIO TRANSMITTER JIGGLES ELECTRONS, SHAKING OFF PHOTONS, WHICH YOU PICK UP WITH YOUR RECEIVER. IN A LIGHT BULB, ELECTRONS IN THE HOT FILAMENT SHAKE OFF VISIBLE LIGHT PHOTONS. AS WE HAVE SEEN FROM THE CLASSICAL THEORY, WHENEVER A CHARGE IS ACCELERATED, AN ELECTROMAGNETIC WAVE — VIRTUAL PHOTONS MADE REAL — RADIATE OUT. MOST OF THE FAMILIAR SOURCES OF RADIATION SHAKE THEIR PHOTONS OUT OF THE VIRTUAL CLOUDS OF CHARGES.

FIRE

FIREFLY

X-RAYS

MICROWAVES

THE BOMB

IF THE QUANTUM THEORY PREDICTED ONLY FAMILIAR EFFECTS, IT WOULDN'T BE MUCH TO GET EXCITED ABOUT. BUT IT DOES MORE: IT ALSO PREDICTS NEW RESULTS.

FOR EXAMPLE, IT IMPLIES TINY DISCREPANCIES FROM THE CLASSICAL THEORY: DEVIATIONS FROM THE INVERSE-SQUARE LAW AT VERY SHORT RANGE, DIFFERENCES IN THE MAGNETIC FIELD OF THE ELECTRON, AND MORE. THESE EFFECTS HAVE BEEN CONFIRMED BY DELICATE EXPERIMENTS, GIVING US CONFIDENCE THAT WE NOW HAVE THE CORRECT THEORY OF THE ELECTROMAGNETIC FORCE.

204

THE WHOLE IDEA OF FORCES BEING CARRIED BY "EXCHANGE
PARTICLES" LIKE PHOTONS HAS BEEN BROADLY EXTENDED IN
PHYSICS. THE PHYSICIST'S MOTTO:

THE **STRONG** NUCLEAR FORCE,
WHICH BINDS PROTONS TOGETHER
IN THE NUCLEUS, IS NOW DESCRIBED
BY AN EXCHANGE OF PARTICLES
CALLED **MESONS**. THE **WEAK**
NUCLEAR FORCE HAS BEEN UNIFIED
TO THE ELECTROMAGNETIC FORCE
BY THEORIZING, AND THEN FINDING,
"BROTHERS" OF THE PHOTON
THAT CARRY THE FORCE.

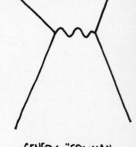

GENERIC "FEYNMAN
DIAGRAM" OF PARTICLE
EXCHANGE

THE FORCE BETWEEN THE QUARKS WHICH MAKE UP THE NEUTRONS
AND PROTONS IS ALSO THEORIZED TO COME FROM THE EXCHANGE
OF PARTICLES CALLED **GLUONS**.

AND GRAVITY...?

AH, GRAVITY... GRAVITY SHOULD BE CAUSED BY THE EXCHANGE OF **GRAVITONS**... BUT WE DON'T EXPECT TO SEE ANY GRAVITONS SOON. THE GRAVITATIONAL FORCE IS JUST TOO WEAK. IT TAKES A WHOLE MOON OR PLANET TO EXERT AN APPRECIABLE GRAVITATIONAL FORCE. BUT WE'RE CONFIDENT THE GRAVITONS ARE "THERE."

GRAVITON
(ENLARGED)

PHYSICISTS STILL BELIEVE THAT ALL THE FORCES
OF NATURE RESULT FROM THE EXCHANGE OF
PARTICLES. BY RELATING THESE PARTICLES,
WE HOPE TO DEVELOP A UNIFIED PICTURE OF
ALL FORCES WITH A SMALL LIST OF RULES
WHICH WILL DESCRIBE THE BASIS OF —
EVERYTHING.

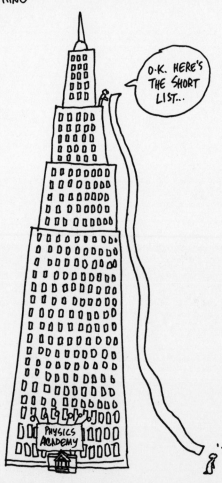